Decline and Fall to Rise and Shine

Decline and Fall

to

Rise and Shine

Nine months in the rebirth of a dying school
in a viral year

Chris Arnot

This edition published 2020 by:
Takahe Publishing Ltd.
Registered Office:
77 Earlsdon Street, Coventry CV5 6EL

Copyright © Chris Arnot 2020

ISBN 978-1-908837-16-5

TAKAHE PUBLISHING LTD. 2020

To those who inspire disadvantaged youngsters
to change their lives for the better

Acknowledgements

Writing a book about a single school on the far west side of Birmingham did not immediately appeal to someone who had spent part of the previous year chronicling cricket festivals from Sussex to Cumbria. So thanks to David Kershaw of the Central Academies Trust for selling me the idea as well as telling me the background story and showing me extensive coverage of what was claimed to be 'the UK's most improved school' in the *Birmingham Mail*.

Thanks also to Director of School Improvement Michael Rennie. Not forgetting his remarkable daughter Clare whom I interviewed in the same coffee bar, albeit on different Saturday mornings.

Headteacher Lee Williams has not only been generous with his time, he has also made me welcome during a year when an unexpected pandemic has put an extraordinary strain on himself, his students and his staff.

I've appreciated the chance to chat to Deputy Headteacher Rajdip Kang, who showed me round the new school just before the lockdown. Not forgetting assistant heads Jane Thompson and Lindsay Greatrix who shared their stories of helping boys and their families badly affected by the said lockdown.

Head of maths Alex Nyarko and head of English Kiran Sandhu took time out of their busy schedules to tell me their own intriguing background stories. And Marie Lowndes-Ford welcomed me into music rooms old and new.

She also gave me the chance to chat to boys with eclectic musical tastes: Gurinder Bunger, Sheni Ojo-Grahams and Finnley Greenway.

I shall never forget my visit to the home of the Smith family to meet former "Lordswoodian" and now Old Etonian James "Cheam-Smith" and his parents. Thanks to them and to Haaris Saghir and his mother

Farah for sharing their stories. Not forgetting Denis Brinzei for meeting me in a park on the other side of town the following day.

Denis was back at Lordswood on a memorable morning in August when his GCSE results were among many worthy of celebration. It was also a pleasure to meet Malvin Omali and his parents as well as Junayd Shamraze, Vrutik Gohel, Dylan Cassidy and his mum.

Handing out the envelopes that day was Ruksana Bi, attendance officer at a school where there are very few absentees.

And, last but by no means least, many thanks to long-term receptionist Jasbinder Thandi for showing me round, sharing her perspective on the many changes she's seen and giving me telling insights into the background story of her family.

You've been a great help, Jas, and I can see why your name is up there at the top of the Lordswood "Hall of Fame".

Contents

Introduction

It felt like a different era in January 2020 when I began researching this book. Facemasks were largely confined to hospital operating theatres and university science laboratories. Shaking hands was not frowned upon. Nor was the occasional hug between friends. (Not by most people anyway.)

Lockdowns?

They happened in prisons.

Coronavirus?

That was something for foreign correspondents to report on. News from China, however, gradually began to spread alarm. How long before the dreaded spread of Covid-19 to these shores?

The first cases were reported late in the following month; more the month after. Many more. So many more, in fact, that the coming of a national emergency was all too evident. Death rates soared. Pubs and shops shut. So did restaurants and cafes, theatres and cinemas.

Schools joined the lockdown on March 18, two days after I'd been given a guided tour of Lordswood Boys' mark two. That brand new building was a reflection of faith in a bright new future for a school that had been failing lamentably only three years previously. The "grand opening" had been postponed until heaven knows when. Only the sons of key workers would be allowed in. The rest would have to depend upon remote learning on-line, often in conditions far from ideal.

Although Lordswood lies in a comparatively posh part of town, its pupils come from the inner-city or the terraced streets of nearby Bearwood and Smethwick. The vast majority are Asian or black.

As one who spent his childhood and adolescence in Birmingham in the 1950s and '60s, I'd witnessed ongoing immigration from the Caribbean and the Indian sub-continent to the city then dubbed "the workshop of the world". There were jobs a-plenty. Menial jobs for the most part.

Coming back to Brum during the university vacation, I took "holiday jobs" everywhere from peaceful cemeteries (yes, I was a teenage gravedigger) to noisy factories. There I witnessed non-white workers doing backbreaking jobs in appalling conditions. During lunchtimes and tea-breaks, I also heard more than enough racist comments from men who didn't work half as hard.

My attitude then was the same as now. Nobody has a choice where they're born or what colour they're born. It's what you make of your life that counts. And to make something of your life in the post-industrial UK of today you need a good education.

In the pages that follow you'll be able to read stories of aspiring students and inspiring teachers. In a diverse city the Lordswood staff have been united in their determination to give would-be achievers a chance in challenging times.

Chapter Four is the story of a talented musician who won a scholarship from Lordswood to Eton. His heritage is part Chinese, part Indian, yet his surname is Smith – or Cheam-Smith, as he now prefers to be called.

In Chapter Eleven is a chance to revel in the joy of a Nigerian family who'd arrived in this country just over three years ago. Their "boy" had achieved such outstanding GCSE grades that he'd been offered the chance to do his A-levels at one of Birmingham's venerable grammar schools.

And in the previous chapter is the first meeting with an engaging lad who'd come from Romania, with his mother but without a word of English. Now he has decent grades in English language and literature. Not forgetting just about every other subject, including a six in the all-important graphics. He desperately wants to study graphic design, not just at A-level but also at university.

Hopefully, that is. And hope is what so many of these boys have been given by a school transformed. At one time they would have been written off as "no-hopers".

We're living through a time when the future is impossible for the most profound of prophets to predict. The only thing that we can say for sure is that without qualifications these boys would have no chance of changing their lives for the better. One of these days, that is, when this wretched viral era becomes part of the past.

We live in hope.

Decline and Fall to Rise and Shine

Chapter One

Sent from Coventry

To quote the final line of Prospero's memorable speech in *The Tempest*, "We are such stuff as dreams are made on and our little life is rounded with a sleep". Hopefully the "sleep" wouldn't be for a while yet in my case. But you never know when you reach a certain age. What I didn't know, just after dawn on a January morn in 2020, was that the Coronavirus would be arriving on our shores shortly. What I did know is that my life was beginning to feel "rounded". The older you become, the more the past comes back.

So here I was on the way to Harborne, the Birmingham suburb where I was born. Not that my parents could afford to live there. Certainly not in that part of Harborne known as Lordswood Road, a broad highway lined with large detached houses, expansive drives and expensive price tags. Around the million-pound mark, since you ask.

At the top end of Lordswood Road is a school called, well, Lordswood. Two schools, to be precise: Lordswood Boys and Lordswood Girls. Same name, very different social backgrounds in terms of the majority of pupils. The boys are far more likely to come from "the other side of the tracks" – or rather the other side of the Hagley Road, the dual carriageway that runs west out of Birmingham, with Edgbaston and Harborne on one side and less salubrious parts of the city on the other.

At the point where Hagley Road crosses the top end of Lordswood Road, the "other side" is Bearwood, adjoined to Smethwick in the Borough of Sandwell. House prices on the rows of terraces running off the high street range from £130,000 to £180,000 or so.

Lee Williams, Headteacher at Lordswood Boys, grew up in one of those houses. Quite a few of his pupils live there now, sometimes in temporary accommodation. Others come from poor parts of the inner-city. Some are travelling to Lordswood from Ladywood, where half the population live below the poverty line.

Around forty per cent of the boys' school's students are Asian, some thirty-eight per cent are African-Caribbean and ten per cent are Eastern European. Another ten per cent are classified as "other". Only two per cent are what you might call "white English".

With just over thirty per cent of the boys achieving passes in Maths and English and with students underachieving at historically low levels, things had reached bottom by 2017. The year-eleven cohort of fewer than one hundred students underachieved against their target grades by almost a thousand grades. They were over eleven grades under target, per student. By 2020, on average, each year-eleven student over-achieved against target by six grades. School outcomes had been remarkable for a third consecutive year. More on that later ...

What made the difference?

The coming of the CAT, otherwise known as the Central Academies Trust, largely made up of Headteachers past and present from Birmingham and Coventry. The school's new sponsors took over in September, 2017, and began work on what would become an historic turnaround.

What you might call the top CAT, or rather Chief Executive Officer of the Trust, is David Kershaw. In the 1980s he had transformed Coundon Court School from a chaotic mess into one of the highest performing comprehensive schools in Coventry. He had since been employed by the Department for Education to sort out failing schools in different parts of the country – including the former secondary modern in Bradford which he'd left with no qualifications whatsoever. "You're a nice lad, David, but you're not very bright," were his own Headteacher's parting words.

He was fourteen at the time. He's now seventy-seven. Still a man haunted by his past. Still determined to give disadvantaged children the chances that he had been denied. A driven man, you might say. And now he was driving me across Birmingham, the city where I'd grown up and where he'd finally scraped into teacher-training college.

I knew all this because I'd ghost-written his autobiography *Thanks Shanks*. It told how he thought he was going to make a living through professional football. How he played for Huddersfield Town's junior side alongside a young shaver called Denis Law. How another legendary Scot called Bill Shankly had taken over the club's management. How Shankly had told Kershaw that he wasn't going to make it as a pro' and he really ought to be a teacher. How he'd paid for him to get the necessary qualifications through a correspondence course called Rapid Results.

What I didn't know until our drive from Coventry to Brum was how close David had come to death five years previously. How a superbug called Necrotising Fasciitis had lodged in his throat. How a young consultant from the Czech Republic had finally performed the delicate task of removing it without severing vital vocal pipes. How David had had to learn to speak again. And write. "They had to build up my muscles after three months lying on my back and being fed through a tube," he told me. "Even holding a pen was difficult. But after losing a year from my professional life, I came back more determined than ever to make a difference."

The difference at Lordswood Boys has been astounding since the Central Academies Trust took the reins. It has gone from being one of the worst performing schools in Birmingham to one of the best. The number of year-eleven students achieving the basic GCSE Level Four pass in maths and English had risen from thirty per cent to seventy per cent within a year of the takeover. Now it's higher still.

Meanwhile, one boy has gone from Lordswood to the sixth-form at Eton, having accumulated eleven GCSEs, including three grade nines and four grade eights. Although his name is James Smith, he is of Chinese and Indian descent and happens to be a accomplished classical guitarist. He also happens to have parents who live on the Harborne side of the Hagley Road. Very unusual.

Haaris Saghir is more typical. He comes from Bordesley Green in inner-city Birmingham and was predicted, at the point where CAT took over, to achieve nothing more than Level 3 in English Language and English Literature. As it turned out, he achieved Level 8 in both, the equivalent of A* in "old money".

Who made the difference?

Step forward and take a bow one christened "the Lionel Messi of the classroom" once she had shown how to bring English Literature alive for boys with very little interest in the subject hitherto. Not that Clare Rennie had any qualifications in teaching. She just came in to help out. After all, her father Michael Rennie is the Director of School Improvement.

Both the Rennies will feature in forthcoming chapters, as will other staff and students mentioned above. All that I knew for now was that the "Lionel Messi of the classroom" didn't want to stay in the classroom. Instead she went off to train as a barrister, much to the frustration of David Kershaw. "She was stunning, a natural," he lamented as the rush-hour traffic finally began to thin out and we headed west up the Hagley Road. "She wanted to be a barrister and that was that. Michael warned me that I'd be lucky if I changed her mind. She's a very determined young woman. A character. She's only around five foot one but I remember seeing her going into a class with a lot of lads who were six foot tall in many cases, and she had them eating out of her hand."

A talent for teaching must run in the family. Her father had been the driving force pushing a Coventry school once performing in the bottom twenty schools in the country, into one of the top twenty. His own father, John Rennie, had been chief adviser in the Education Department at Coventry City Council. Rennie senior had come from Manchester. Kershaw had come from Bradford. Both were committed to comprehensive education. Both had worked on transforming

Coundon Court from a chaotic mess to a big success under David's headship.

The entrance to Lordswood appeared suddenly on the left as we approached a building known as the King's Head. Dating from 1898, it had briefly been an Indian restaurant with a different name. Now it had reverted to being a pub again, albeit with an "Indian grill".

Things change. That's life. Lordswood was a technical-grammar school when it came into being in September, 1957. You had to pass the eleven-plus to be admitted. I vaguely remember coming here for a cross-country running fixture sometime in the early sixties.

In those days Birmingham was divided into grammar schools and secondary moderns. As one of only two boys in our road to pass the eleven-plus exam, I was duly despatched to one of several King Edward's foundation grammars spread across the city. Had to wear a uniform, the cause of much mirth among my mates, and endure occasional beatings from be-gowned "masters" who wielded rulers and size eleven plimsolls with relish and, in some cases, belted you over the back of the head to enforce discipline.

The King Edward's foundation, but thankfully not the punishment system, has survived to this day. As a result, there are still grammar schools in various parts of the city. Independent schools too, needless to say, including the original King Edward's School in Edgbaston where annual fees are not too far short of £14,000 a year. "So the wealthier parents in Harborne have other options," David pointed out. "Either they fork out for posh private schools in Edgbaston or they pay for private tutors to train them to get through the eleven-plus."

As we turned off the Hagley Road, there was a sign for Lordswood Boys' School above the motto "learn, believe, succeed". Another sign nearby proclaimed in large capital blue letters "MASSIVE IMPROVEMENT in GCSE results".

The driveway was lined with drills and diggers, and beyond were men in yellow jackets and hard hats. Behind the 1950s building, a new Lordswood Boys' School was rising fast and due to open in early March. New classrooms, updated science laboratories, extensive sports facilities.

It was time to look at the present and future for Lordswood boys, many of whom have had little in their lives so far. Enough of dwelling on the past – for the time being at least.

David Kershaw, chief executive officer of the Central Academies Trust

Sign of hope

Decline and Fall to Rise and Shine

Chapter Two

First Impressions

There were flags: lots of them attached to the ceiling just beyond the school's reception area. Appropriate enough, perhaps, for a school with students whose origins are from all over the globe. Down at ground level were eight shelves full of books written in English. "We will READ, READ, READ," urged a shelf-side sign. Another proclaimed: "Targets are there to be beaten. Aim high."

The office of Headteacher Lee Williams was nearby. A youthful-looking thirty-seven, he started here as an art teacher in 2005 and, unlike quite a few long-term staff members, he has survived and thrived under the Central Academies Trust. "What we saw in him first and foremost was a commitment to the students," I'd been told by David – or "Dr Kershaw" as I should perhaps refer to him now that we were on school premises.

As for Mr Williams, whom we'll be talking to at length in the next chapter, he was brought up in a terraced house on the other side of the Hagley Road. So was Jasbinder Thandi, the receptionist who had been designated to take me on a tour around what might be termed the "old school" in order to gain a few first impressions.

Jas has been working at Lordswood Boys for thirty-eight years. Born into a Sikh family in Smethwick, she converted to Christianity at a difficult time in her life and helped to run the school's Christian Union for many years. She welcomed me warmly, holding out an immaculately manicured and bejewelled right hand before leading the way to the corridors beyond.

It was too early for anybody to be in the "dining room". But a quick glance around gave an indication of how much things have changed since "school dinners" included disgusting spam fritters and were always served with lumpy spuds. Not to mention puddings smothered with thick-skinned custard that had to be forced down while we school "diners" were wedged together on long benches.

Here there were round tables, some of them only accessible by high stools of the sort found in coffee bars. As for the walls, they were bedecked by impressive black and white photos. Done by year-eleven boys apparently, they showed forks and can-openers in a new light – or at least a clever use of lighting. "There are some very talented boys here," Jas confirmed.

On to the music room where one class was leaving and another arriving, somewhat discordantly. Boys are boisterous. Always have been, always will be. But they soon quietened down and settled down. High on the walls were pictures of, among others, the Beatles, the Beach Boys and The Rolling Stones.

My youth.

"At the moment," said the lead music teacher Marie Lowndes-Ford, "we're looking at the history of 1950s rock 'n' roll."

My childhood.

"I'm a teacher who believes that music is for everybody," Ms Lowndes-Ford went on. "Some boys have started violin lessons with me and I'm taking my year-seven boys on a trip to the Symphony Hall to listen to and see the CBSO [City of Birmingham Symphony Orchestra]."

"Will they like that?" I enquired.

"Oh yes."

She was right, if the three lads that I chatted with soon after the concert were anything to go by. "It was great," said eleven-year-old Gurinder Bunger who was born in Rome of Indian parents and who now lives in Handsworth. "That visit will stay with me. All the children were talking until they turned the lights down and the orchestra started playing. The music was based on stories. When one finished, the conductor told us another one."

"They were also using music to give us feelings," put in Sheni Ojo-Grahams, who's twelve but seems older. "Sometimes music makes you happy, sometimes sad. I liked how the orchestra used such a range of instruments and followed what the conductor was signalling. I sometimes listen to Classic FM," added Sheni, who was born two miles up the other side of the Hagley Road in Winson Green. "Both my parents came from Nigeria and we now live in Edgbaston – the all-right part rather than the posh part."

Finnley Greenway, also twelve, comes from Quinton on the far west side of Birmingham and is one of very few Lordswood boys with white parents born in England. Just about in the case of his father, who came from this side of the Scottish border.

Enjoys a bit of classical music does Finnley. "I was in the Merry Hill Shopping Centre once and somebody was playing the piano. I asked him what the song was and he said, 'It's not a song; it's a piece by Mozart.' I liked it. Still do. I sometimes play it on my phone in my bedroom when I'm a bit bored."

He also likes a "bit of drill and a bit of rap". And, like the other two, he'd heard of the Beatles. "*Hey Jude* was one of their songs," he reminded me. "And *We All Live in a Yellow Submarine*."

Not the greatest work by the Beatles, perhaps. And not quite up there with Mozart's 21st Piano Concerto, whether or not you heard it in the Symphony Hall or the Merry Hill Shopping Centre.

Time to listen to a bit of Jas, perhaps, as my school tour continued. As we left the music room, crammed with keyboards and sets of drums, she told me about her nephew's days at Lordswood before the arrival of the Central Academies Trust. "The teachers weren't there for him, particularly in his last year. Some were always going off sick. Supply teachers were coming in and some of them didn't know what they were supposed to be doing. Thankfully, he got through it because he had a good strong family behind him, and he's now a chartered accountant.

"It's not like that here now. The teachers are pushing them. What I like about Mr Rennie is his philosophy that education is the most important thing in life. It gives you the chance to make a better life for yourself and your family. The new regime wants these boys to get somewhere. I really support them."

As she was talking, we passed spelling tests and messages pasted to corridor walls. One message was from Barrack Obama: "Literacy is the most basic currency of the knowledge economy." Another proclaimed that "Education is our passport for the future, for tomorrow belongs to the people who prepare for it today".

That was Malcolm X, founder of the Black Power movement, who caused quite a stir when he turned up in Smethwick in 1965. "I have come," he told the press, "because I am disturbed by reports that coloured people in Smethwick are being treated badly. I have heard that they are being treated as the Jews were under Hitler."

A startling statement, to put it mildly, and yes he did use the term "coloured people". The local MP Peter Griffiths, a Tory populist born locally, had defied the national trend by winning the parliamentary seat the previous year thanks to a far more objectionable term. "If you want a nigger for a neighbour, vote Labour," were the posters that appeared in many a front window.

Jas was only seven at the time of Malcolm X's visit and, not surprisingly, she remembers nothing about it. She does, though, recall the racism that was par for the course in her school days. How a gang of white boys picked on her brother, calling him "Paki" and beating him up in the local park. How she and her sister were "ignored as if we were nobodies" when they put up their hands to answer questions in the classroom.

Smethwick had seemed a lot more tolerant when Spike Lee's film about Malcolm X was released in 1993 and I went there to write an article for *The Independent* about the Black Power leader's visit nearly thirty years previously. Bearing in mind his comments about Hitler and the treatment of the Jews, I'd concluded the piece with the line, "Malcolm X did not live long enough to know that the biggest concentration of ovens in Smethwick is in the gas showrooms on Bearwood Road."

Another nigh-on thirty years on and the Far Right has made something of a comeback in a post-Brexit world bedevilled by abuse on-line as well as in person. Luckily, there are plenty of individuals and institutions determined to counter those retrograde trends. This school is one of them. That became ever more evident every time Jas and I stepped out of a corridor and into a classroom. The welcome was warm, be the subject music or art, maths or English. Or German for that matter.

Some of the boys hardly had any knowledge of English before they arrived at Lordswood. So why did they need to learn German?

"It's a good add-on to the curriculum because it's a high-order thinking skill," I was assured by Lindsay Greatrix, Assistant Headteacher, who was taking a class with few empty desks. "This school constantly stresses the importance of literacy and we read in German as well as talk. We've had a good uptake and there are twenty-six in the year-ten class."

The woman responsible for ensuring that classes are reasonably full, whatever the subject, just happened to have called into today's German lesson. "Attendance Officer" is Ruksana Bi's title and her faith is evidently Muslim, judging by her dress and headgear. A hijab rather than a niqab, mind you. No veil in other words.

"I have to keep track of all the boys," she told me, "and make sure that they're in school every day. We have an attendance record of something like ninety-seven per cent. It helps that we give rewards out, mainly vouchers that can be used on Amazon for everything from education resources to music. But, to be honest, the vast majority *know* that they have to be here every day. Lack of attendance leads to lack of progress. That in itself is a big incentive."

As Jas reminded me when we were out in the corridor once more, "What they're doing at this school is trying to change lives. Some of the boys here have had to battle against real hardship." As if to emphasise the point, she introduced me to Jane Thompson, a senior history teacher and Assistant Headteacher who is also responsible for "safeguarding" – coordinating measures to ensure a safer school and protect vulnerable children.

"I have to work with external agencies such as Social Services," she stressed. "Some of the students come from very challenging circumstances. Many of the recently arrived ones are living in temporary accommodation in parts of the city with high crime rates."

So why do they come to school in this comparatively posh part of town?

"Partly because we had many empty places and some of the inner-city schools are oversubscribed. And over the past couple of years I think we're beginning to gain a good reputation when it comes to supporting children with a different language from English. We're also markedly improving academically. Hopefully that will begin to draw in more boys from the local area," she added before going on to say, "The boys here are wonderful. They really are. Some of them have overcome real hardship."

That could also be said of some of the teachers. Somewhere near a corridor with a poster urging us to learn to spell words such as "column", "actually", "moreover", "Saturday" and "Wednesday", Kiran Sandhu was all too evidently in full command of a diligent year-eleven English class. "They're the top set," she assured me. "At the moment they're revising for their mock GCSE and a quarter of their exams will be made up of fifteen poems that they need to know inside out."

Blake's *London* and Tennyson's *Charge of the Light Brigade* are part of the curriculum. A bit of Wilfred Owen too. Well, this is the Power and Conflict syllabus. "We could have had the love poems instead. But this is a boys' school. Love or conflict? Wonder which one they're going to prefer?" the head of English mused smilingly.

Miss Sandhu we must call her, as all female teachers are "Miss-es", even if they're a "Mrs" or a "Ms" beyond the school gates. She had started life in inner-city Aston, not too far from the Villa ground, and soon found herself in a one-parent family. Her mother had been born into a Sikh family in India and moved to England when she was five. Like Jas, she had still been expected to go through with an arranged marriage. Unlike Jas, hers had ended in a "messy divorce" when Kiran was four and her sister eight. "Mum" would eventually become an accountant. "But at one point she couldn't afford to pay the bills to keep the house and we ended up sleeping in one room so that she could rent out the other two. I think that's what made me so driven, so ambitious to make a better life."

She started reading while sitting on the stairs for some peace and quiet. Enid Blyton at first before moving on to somewhat more demanding books. And, yes, she made it into one of the King Edwards grammar schools: Rose Hill in Handsworth. Taught at one too: Five Ways in Bartley Green (my old school, as it happened).

But she'd cut her teaching teeth at a tough comprehensive near where she'd been brought up. "There was a fight on my first day between two boys who seemed to be about six foot four," she recalled. "I had to step in between them."

Miss Sandhu came to Lordswood under the new regime in 2018 and is evidently relishing the challenges thrown up by introducing Blake, Tennyson and Shakespeare to boys who, in quite a few cases, have arrived in "this sceptred isle" comparatively recently.

"One boy I teach in year-ten is a refugee from the Sudan with no family here apart from his brother. He sleeps on a mattress after travelling long distances on boats, via France and Spain. You'd never imagine the horror stories that he's seen, yet he's one of the most studious of the boys. He comes here on time every day with a smile on his face, eager to learn."

Alex Nyarko, Subject Team Leader for Maths, came to the UK from Ghana eager to teach. And he has succeeded, judging by the atmosphere of studious silence that prevailed when Jas and I looked in on his year-ten class. Heads were down. Brains were evidently whirring. Not wishing to interrupt, I accepted Jas's whispered confirmation that he was "a very good teacher".

Luckily I was given the chance to chat to Mr Nyarko later. He'd arrived in the UK when the new century dawned and new opportunities beckoned. "I wanted to further my own education," he explained. "Although I'd taught in Ghana, I had to re-train for a year at university because the system here in the UK is very different. There it was more about telling the boys what to do. Here you have to draw it out of them. Also it's much more diverse here. Back home you might have a couple of families from Britain or America, but most of the class would be Ghanaian."

With a somewhat more deferential attitude towards teachers, it would seem.

"There was respect," he confirmed. "If they saw you in a supermarket after school, for instance, they'd rush over and carry your groceries to the car."

Not surprisingly, he was somewhat nervous when he started teaching at Lordswood Girls after his year at university. "It seemed quite demanding because the students were far more advanced by year-eleven than they had been in Ghana."

Teaching at the school next door after a spell at a mixed-gender academy in north Birmingham proved demanding in a different way. "When I started here in 2013, the boys' behaviour was terrible."

"So how did you cope?"

"I tried to understand their backgrounds. How did I get to their needs? Once I understood that, it gave me a lead. I worked out which ones needed spoon-feeding and which ones could work things out independently. The really disruptive ones had to be sent to the isolation centre for one-to-one monitoring. But then a lot of the boys had no stable home. I found out that one boy ran to school and back, quite a few miles, because he was never given any money for the bus. He had a free school meal here, but I'm fairly sure he wasn't getting much to eat at home. I worked really hard with him in the classroom and he'd changed markedly by the time he left."

Mr Nyarko has also come across some "inspirational maths", it would seem, from students who could hardly speak English when they arrived here. "One Romanian boy can do it just like that," he said, snapping his fingers, before going on to add that "it's a joy to teach here now".

Presumably it was the coming of the CAT that made the difference. The Central Academies Trust in other words.

"It was," he confirmed. "They gave us authority, put us in charge. The 'deal' about not pushing the boys too hard was over."

To learn more about that deal it was time to talk to someone born and brought up just across the Hagley Road; someone with a long term perspective on Lordswood Boys' School.

Time to find the Headteacher's office.

Jasbinder Thandi, school receptionist for thirty-eight years

Assistant head Jane Thompson in the classroom before the lockdown

Chapter Three

Local Boy Made Head

My expectations of coffee in other people's workplaces are not high. But on this occasion I was presented not with something spooned from a jar into boiling water and UHT milk. Instead there came an Americano, black and strong with a proper "crema". A head, in other words. And the head, in a different sense of the word, was the one who had just brought over two cups from a steaming machine in the corner of his office.

In the circumstances it was not a great surprise when Lee Williams revealed that the idea of attendance vouchers had come to him in a coffee bar. After all, chains such as Caffe Nero have long handed out cards to be stamped every time you order something from the barista. Once you've accumulated so many stamps, you're offered a free espresso, latte, cappuccino or whatever.

"We now have our own loyalty card for year-eleven students," explained the Headteacher, whipping one out of his pocket. "When a student goes to an extra-curricular intervention session* after school or at lunchtimes, they get the equivalent of a stamp – a teacher's signature. And when they fill the card up, they can cash it in for a £10 Amazon gift card."

More gift cards are available through a regular grand draw for students from all years. The ones entered are those with an attendance level of over ninety-six per cent.

Not too many truants among Lordwood Boys these days. "Yet they're from diverse backgrounds and from socially deprived areas all over the inner-city and beyond," the head reflected. "The social deprivation has got worse and worse since I started here in 2005."

*An extra-curricular intervention session is typically used to improve English and maths, key double-counting subjects in the GCSE outcomes.

In those distant days he was a young art teacher of twenty-two. And unlike many of his students, his roots were not half way across the world. They were just across the road – the Hagley Road that is. He was brought up about a three-minute walk from the school in a row of terraces just off Bearwood High Street. "Mind you, I didn't know that Lordswood existed until I was working at Safeway and met some friends who went here," he recalled.

Yes, Safeway the supermarket. Needless to say, that was a weekend-cum-holiday job. He was in his teens at the time and, having been to a local comprehensive school, he was doing A-levels at a sixth-form college in nearby Rowley Regis. Then it was on to the University of Central England in Birmingham for courses in communication studies and graphic design.

"Didn't you fancy going away to study?" I asked after savouring another flavoursome sip of coffee.

"No, I haven't moved far from this area. I'm quite committed to it."

Admittedly, he did have a brief spell in London. After graduating with an upper-second in 2003, he was employed by Saatchi and Saatchi. Yes, the advertising agency that rocketed to prominence in with the "Labour isn't working" poster credited with helping to win the general election of 1979 for one Margaret Thatcher. Mind you, that was four years before Lee. . . sorry, Mr Williams, was born.

"I was only working there and in other advertising agencies as an unpaid intern," he reflected. "It was a useful experience and it went on just long enough to make me realise that this wasn't a business that I wanted to stay in. There was a lack of much in the way of any moral standpoint."

Where, I wondered, had his own moral values come from?

"My family was nominally Christian, but we didn't regularly attend church. I did, though, have amazing parents. Mum was canteen manager at a local primary school and Dad was a fireman. Salt of the earth."

Dig deep, aim high. Whether or not the family had a motto, those seem to have been the values that the head has inherited. On one of his office walls is photograph of the L'Alpe d'Huez, 3,330 metres above sea level at its highest point. That's 10,925 feet for those of us brought up with furlongs and chains, rods, poles and perches on the back of our school exercise books – measurements that may well make a comeback if the more ardent Brexiteers get their way.

I digress.

Beneath the photo are the words "It's only a failure if you stop trying. Right now it's just an experience." One of the remaining Williams ambitions is evidently to cycle up that mountain one of these days. "I always take my bike on holiday in the Pyrenees," he confided. And even when he's not on holiday, he seems to think nothing of pounding the pedals for around one hundred miles. That's when he has a bit of time at weekends. During the week he's far too busy overseeing a school of nearly four hundred students. With more to come as its reputation rises, a new building opens and a new dawn beckons.

Time perhaps to return to the tale of Lee Williams's move into education:

After his short dalliance with the world of advertising, he returned to Birmingham and teamed up with one of his former lecturers. "I had a lot of faith in his outlook with regard to design and creativity," said the head. "And he always had a connection with Gallery 37 – an arts project for disadvantaged local youths. So I enrolled on the programme and, for six weeks in the summer of 2004, we put up a temporary space in Centenary Square and invited teenagers to come and work with resident artists and art graduates.

"Not only did I meet some amazing people; I came out on the other side being offered all kinds of artist-in-residence projects from primary and secondary schools around the city on a freelance basis. And at the end of that year I had another conversation with my former lecturer who suggested that I should apply to do a PGSE (Post Graduate Certificate of Education). He also suggested the best place to do it – the School of Art, a stunning building on Margaret Street with a well-renowned programme. From then on my outlook on education was just transformed. I was hungry to help develop creative links within schools."

The link with Lordswood came on a Monday morning when he returned to lectures after a weekend at the Download Festival where that old Brummie heavy metal basher Ozzie Osbourne had been the major attraction. Here I should point out that the young Lee Williams, no less, was the lead vocalist in a heavy metal band called Random Conflict. They toured the UK and Europe a number of times and made more than one album.

Emma Thacker was somewhat quieter as the visiting lecturer on that Monday morning at the School of Art. At the time she was Lordswood's Subject Team Leader for Art and, it transpired, she had a job vacancy for someone with good IT and graphical skills. To cut a long story short, she was the one who interviewed the future Headteacher "in this very room".

She was also the one who gave him the job. "Emma and I are still friends to this day. She rose through the ranks to become Assistant Headteacher before moving on to do other things."

His own rise through the ranks hasn't stopped him taking art classes. "I still do six hours a week, which I think is unusual for a head." Then again he gives the impression of being someone who would enjoy being back at what used to be known as "the chalk-face". Perhaps the "paint-face" might be a more appropriate term in this case.

He is also a man who, by his own admission, likes to push himself. He had been assistant head for four years or so and had felt "like a minority voice" when, to use his own words, "there were clear signs that things weren't going right coupled with an inability to change anything".

There must have been times when he had felt like moving on to another job elsewhere. Had he considered that?

"No. I've always been committed to this school. The students have deserved so much more. I'd never say that I've found my job easy. But I enjoy unlocking the abilities of these boys and helping them to understand that they're a lot cleverer than they give themselves credit for."

Two influential figures helped Lee Williams to understand that he could take a major role in helping to make major changes at Lordswood Boys. One was Michael Rennie, Director of School Improvement for the Central Academies Trust (see Chapter Six). "Michael transformed my perspective with regard to the school and was able to draw out some inner abilities that he apparently saw in my character that would allow leadership skills to develop."

The other key figure who helped him to believe that he had what it takes was his wife Kelly. "She's been as influential as Michael in giving me the self-belief to progress my career," he reflected. Kelly works for the Department for Works and Pensions when she's not looking after their three children, aged three, six and ten, at their home in Erdington, an all too cycle-able eight and a half miles from Lordswood.

My conversation with the Headteacher had taken place shortly before the opening of the nearby new school building designed to meet the educational needs of the 21st century rather than the middle of the 20th.

"You can teach students anywhere," Lee mused. "But certain environments provide different opportunities. We have Science labs here in the 'old school' that were built in the late 1950s. Yet Science teaching has developed and changed over time. There are all kinds of new technologies that can be better explored in a new setting. And there'll also be better performance spaces and sports fields. A new environment can change attitudes. It's also somewhere that the local community will be encouraged to spend time in as often as possible."

Does that mean attracting people from Harborne side of the Hagley Road --those who send their sons to independent schools or pay for private tutors to boost their chances of passing the eleven-plus?

"Exactly. We'll have new football pitches, sports hall and a pavilion and court that are part of the Edgbaston Priory Tennis Club." An exclusive club, to be sure, with its headquarters in a leafy part of town. Yet in this Lordswood outpost it's allowing the use of its facilities to boys from Smethwick, Ladywood and Winson Green. Harborne boys, it would seem, are still very much a minority among the students. "But because of the school's markedly improved reputation," Mr Williams pointed out, "we're getting more than we've had in recent history."

Certainly more than when James Smith first arrived here in 2013 from his home on the leafy borders of Harborne and Edgbaston. "Not only was he very bright academically," the head recalled. "He was also an unbelievably talented classical guitarist. Absolutely phenomenal."

James was now eighteen and still studying as well as stroking the strings. Not at a Birmingham grammar school and not at a local sixth-form college, however. During term-time at least, he was much closer to Windsor in Berkshire. At somewhere called Eton College.

This was a story that I needed to know more about. Luckily I managed to catch up with James and his parents when he was briefly back home for half-term. Yes, they'd be happy to chat. No, I didn't have the car on the afternoon of our meeting. It was time to catch the train and then "ger on the buz", as they used to say in Birmingham (but not Windsor), and meet up with a remarkable family.

The gateway to Sandwell where headteacher Lee Williams grew up and many a Lordswood pupil still lives

Lee Williams with renewed pride in the Lordswood logo

Chapter Four

From Lordswood to Eton

As usual in Birmingham there was work going on. Building works in one part, road works in another. Accordingly, the number 24 seemed to take an eternity to travel via various diversions from the centre of town a couple of miles westward to Five Ways. The ongoing journey through the Edgbaston that has always prospered behind the Hagley Road was comparatively plain bussing. Grand houses, ancient churches, expensive restaurants and private schools came into view.

After gazing with fond nostalgia at the gateway to plant-packed greenhouses and green spaces of the Botanical Gardens, I alighted on Harborne Road and spent the next twenty minutes trying to find the address that young Etonian James Smith had texted from his phone. Another text arrived as time ticked away and James came out to find me.

The family home turned out to be a two-bedroomed flat in a low-storey 1970s block, tucked away at the bottom of a cul-de-sac surrounded by mature trees. No fewer than five school friends from Eton have been overnight visitors here since James won a scholarship from Lordswood when he was sixteen in 2018.

"They came one at a time during school holidays," his mother Julie assured me. "At first I thought 'oh my gosh, why has he invited them'? Did I have to curtsy or bow? These were boys from very wealthy backgrounds, almost all of them from London. But as it turned out, they were lovely and very polite."

"I took them to the middle of Birmingham," James put in, "and, much to my surprise, they seemed to like it. We even went to Wetherspoon's."

At this point I must have looked slightly agog or amused, but I restrained from asking if there was a "decent claret" available. James was also grinning broadly when he went on to say, "Yes, I thought you might get a bit of Etonian snobbery. But when the tailcoat comes off they're just ... "

The words tailed away, possibly because James saw me peering at a photograph of himself on the mantelpiece, sporting a tailcoat with a waistcoat and a shirt with a what looked like a very high collar. A detachable collar, apparently. "That's what I have to wear when I'm there," he shrugged.

How he came to be "there" at the school that has produced no fewer than twenty British prime ministers straight from a comprehensive that had been in special measures soon after he arrived is a story that we shall get to shortly. For now it's worth explaining how a boy called Smith, the most English of surnames, grew up with a heritage that could best be described as diverse.

Julie's parents were Chinese. She was born in Edinburgh, grew up in Newcastle and moved to Birmingham as a student nurse in 1984. "I met Glen a couple of years later," she said, gesturing towards her husband. "We were next-door neighbours."

Glen, now sixty-two and a learning support assistant in a local college, was just one year old when he came to Birmingham from India. He was born to a Nepalese mother and an Indian father. "Dad was an accountant," he confided. Which may explain why they could afford to live in Harborne. What it doesn't explain is why such a family was called Smith. Something to do with an Irish great grandfather apparently. Maybe he came from Northern Ireland where Smiths are not unknown.

James's middle name is Cheam, from his mother's side of the family. He uses it as part of his email address and is planning to have his surname changed to Cheam-Smith. Note the hyphen. "It seems more distinguished," he explained.

Well, certainly double-barrelled names are more common at Eton than at Lordswood. And talking of Lordswood, it was time to ask an obvious question to the parents of a boy whose brain-power must have been evident from an early age: "Why did you want him to go there?"

"We didn't," they chorused before Julie went on to say, "He didn't get the eleven-plus because he missed a page."

The normally genial James looked almost pained at this point, as one reminded of something that he'd rather forget. "I didn't turn over when I should have done." He shook his head before going on to admit that "it was traumatising to hear that I hadn't passed. I'd put in so much work. It really knocked my confidence when I found out."

The school he had expected to go to was King Edward's Five Ways. Yes, it had been founded at the Five Ways that I mentioned earlier, on the western edge of the city centre. But no it hasn't been located there for many a year. It had already relocated to the outer suburb of Bartley Green by the time that I first went there in 1960 after dismounting at the 18 bus terminal and then trudging across what seemed like a vast and blustery reservoir.

It always was much easier to get to by bus from the Harborne and Edgbaston side of town, and it seems likely that James would have thrived there over half a century later. After all he has a head bulging with brains and fingers capable of turning a guitar into an instrument of great subtlety.

"He used to do a bit of rehearsing by the canteen at Lordswood," Glen smiled. "And quite a few of the 'dinner ladies' would sit and listen."

Not a guarantee of lunch always being served on time, perhaps, but gratifying for a budding musician. So come on, James, tell us what Lordswood was like in other respects when you moved there from Harborne Junior School some six or seven years ago.

"To be honest, it was not the best learning environment. I remember vividly writing an essay while there must have been a fight going on in the corridor outside. Two boys crashed through the door and landed on my desk. The first three years or so were a struggle. It was nothing like the school it is now. But I made some good friendships. All three of my best friends from there are Pakistani. They think it's hilarious that I'm at Eton, especially when they Skype me and see me in that high collar and bow tie."

Considering the problems of those early years at Lordswood, it's quite remarkable that he came out with no fewer than eleven GCSE passes, including three grade nines and four grade eights. Those would have been single or double-starred 'A's under the old system. Bear in mind that in 2017, his penultimate year, only thirty per cent of boys on the year above him were achieving level four in maths and English — the "just about passed" level in other words.

Enter the Central Academies Trust.

"For the last year or so I felt that I was working together with the teachers," James recalled. "They were almost like colleagues." A marked contrast for sure with those "first few years" when, as he put it, "some of the teachers were just babysitting the pupils, trying to make sure that they were behaving reasonably well. At that time there would be a significant number of staff leaving at the end of each term and a lot of temporary teachers standing in for them."

Apart from his academic prowess, young Smith had plucked ninety-seven out of one hundred in the Trinity College music exam. That's a top grade of eight. Oh yes, and he'd become lead player in the Birmingham Schools Guitar Ensemble and lead bass player in the National Youth Guitar Ensemble, performing at venues such as the Royal Overseas League in London and the Yehudi Menuhin School in Surrey.

Take a bow Liz Larner, his music teacher since he was at Harborne Primary, aged nine. Having graduated with honours from the Royal Birmingham Conservatoire in 2003, she still lives in the city but has travelled across Europe to perform for music societies and festivals. Closer to home, she has also played in various seasons at the Royal Shakespeare Company and now teaches music at Edgbaston High School as well as the nearby King Edward VI High School for Girls.

The Smiths carried on paying for her services as James's private tutor during his time at Lordswood. Music was not an option on the boys' side. "James had to go next door to the girls' school during his time there," Julie remembered. "He had to rejig some of his lessons and catch up in his own time. At that time he really wanted to study music. He had a passion for it and wanted a career in it. He also wanted to go to boarding school."

The obvious solution was a music school that offered boarding – Cheethams in Manchester, perhaps? That hit all the right notes. But, alas, you'd need a hell of a lot of notes in your bank account to be able to afford it.

"So I looked on Google for musical scholarships and Eton came up," Julie went on. "He met all the criteria with his grades. But he had to audition for two or three pieces to show that he could play competently in public."

Over to you again, James:

"I had to go down to Eton for three days. In that time I had eight interviews, three exams and had to play in front of the head of music, the guitar teacher and another music teacher."

There followed a two-week wait that seemed like an eternity. Cue laughter from all three when I asked how they heard. "There was no letter at first," Julie explained. "And when I checked my emails on the December day that we were due to hear, I couldn't find anything. I remember thinking to myself, 'Oh my God, he didn't get in'. Then Glen had a look and found it. I remember holding my breath before letting out a huge sigh on hearing that he had his scholarship and we didn't have to pay anything."

It's an academic as well as musical scholarship, as James pointed out. "I'm doing German and English as well as music."

Just as well, perhaps. "Music in an academic way is very strenuous," he went on. "It's my hardest A-level by far. I've decided that, eventually, I'd prefer to do it as a leisure-time pursuit."

Glen made a rare intervention at this point. "We shelled out two and a half thousand quid for a special guitar when we knew he was going to Eton," he almost sighed.

Julie shrugged. "It's still there and he still plays it. It's just that he's decided that he doesn't want to specialise in music." Time, perhaps, to change the subject and ask James how he felt when he clapped eyes on his "new" school.

"I'll never forget the first time that we drove down there. The first thing I saw was the chapel. We were still some way away but my heart stopped. It's the most breath-taking scene. I don't think I could have imagined it looking as good as it did."

Any apprehension about being accepted into what is widely regarded as the grandest of UK public schools?

"To begin with I was a bit nervous. Then you realise that Eton boys are still boys. I've met some lovely people and have some great friends there. Boarding together is almost like having another family. I settled in within a few weeks."

With all those posh white boys?

"That's a bit of a misconception. There are also Chinese and other races as well. It's getting more and more diverse."

Any bullying?

"Nothing physical. It's just a few snarky comments now and again. I think because you live together you have to get used to each other. And, no, we don't share a dormitory. You have your own room."

He is in the sixth-form after all, doing A-levels so I presumed.

"At Eton they're called 'Pre-U's,'" James corrected me. The "U", needless to say, stands for university. "Oxford or Cambridge?" I enquired, somewhat presumptuously.

"I have an unconditional offer to go to Lancaster," he said. "I'm thinking of doing German as a main course with Italian and management."

Why not Oxbridge?

"Because I suspect that Oxford or Cambridge would be very similar to Eton," he mused before quickly adding, "Don't get me wrong. I love being there and, as I said, I have a lot of good friends there."

I sensed a "but" coming. Instead there was a slight sigh.

"Sometimes it's so academically pushing. I'd like just to go to a normal university. And Lancaster's something like seventh in the national league tables. What's more, my sister Jess is not too far away in Liverpool, doing a PhD in psychology."

Was he having qualms about "the system"? I wondered out loud.

Another sigh. "Er … yes."

So what would he like to see in an ideal world?

"I don't think it's possible to have an ideal world. Starting at Lordswood and seeing that side of things before going to Eton where everything sometimes seems so gold-plated … well, you just see how unfair it is. Mind you, that's something I should really bite my tongue about. I feel really ungrateful just thinking it. Oh my gosh, just think where I've come to, I tell myself."

What about abolishing public schools (and grammar schools for that matter) and having an entirely comprehensive system?

"I'm not sure that would be good either. Eton is doing more and more educational outreach to spread its resources. There's now another scholarship called the Orwell Award."

A reminder there that the great writer who took *The Road to Wigan Pier* after being *Down and Out in Paris and London* was himself an Old Etonian.

James would be returning to that fabled school in a couple of days. For me it was time to say goodbye to that charming lad and his hospitable family. Heading back to the bus stop through the enclave of trees around their flat, I found myself reflecting on the past. Again.

After leaving the grammar school that he would have attended were it not for a missed page, I scraped into the university that he should sail into. Sometime during the so-called "Summer of Love" in 1967, I was offered a place at Lancaster after being on the "waiting list". My A-level results had somewhat exceeded expectations. Particularly those of the "master" who'd once written on my school report, "Wish he could bring to his work the enthusiasm that characterises his cricket."

Enough.

Time, once again, to concentrate on the future. While James returned to his very old new school, I would soon be setting off for the grand opening of his old school's new building. Or so I thought.

****

Three weeks after meeting James, his time at Eton came to an end all too suddenly. Having returned to school on Sunday March 15 after a weekend "exeat", he was sent home again. Had a bit of a cough and that couldn't be risked at a time when the threat from the Coronavirus had dawned with a vengeance.

"My 'dame' [Eton word for the house matron] suggested that I should stay at home for seven days," James told me by email. There is nothing like a dame, it would seem, to look after the welfare of Etonian boys. No arguing with a dame either, I should imagine.

"During the week I was at home," James went on, "there were daily updates on the virus and, by the end of the week, College had closed for the foreseeable future."

Most of his clothes were still there. So was his beloved guitar as well as other belongings.

"So my dad and I drove down to clear out my room. It took a while but, to be honest, I really regretted having rushed home at the beginning of that weekend break and not really absorbing what was around me. While Dad packed the car, I had one last walk around the house, taking pictures on my phone and admittedly letting a few little tears come out."

Birmingham beckoned. And he'd been back there ever since. Weeks had passed by the time we exchanged emails. Many thousands had died in the meantime, in this country alone. And thousands more had come close to death, including our Old Etonian Prime Minister. While Boris lavished praise on the NHS staff who had cared for him at St Thomas's Hospital in London, many more doctors and nurses all over the country were putting themselves on the line every day. Including James's mother Julie.

"I know my mum is struggling a bit from the stress of work," the email confirmed, after admitting that "if boredom is my biggest worry during a pandemic outbreak, I'm quite lucky."

Plenty of academically stimulating course work was still coming in on-line from Eton. And more in the form of "niche topics", such as ancient Chinese philosophy and African theology, to keep the academic antennae tuned in. Nonetheless, it was hardly the same as being there.

"I do miss so much about it," James admitted. "The opportunities there are unparalleled and something I took for granted: the chance to go out spontaneously on an evening and watch a semi-professional house play, participate in a society, enjoy the music performances of fellow students. More than that, though, I miss seeing friends and living in the hustle and bustle of a boarding house shared by fifty-five boys.

"Long essays and short deadlines? I don't miss them at all."

He would go back to Eton for social occasions, eventually. Nobody knew when. The annual 'Fourth of June' celebrations had been postponed. It would happen one day, perhaps. So would his German teachers' Kaffee and Kuchen (coffee and cake) afternoon, followed by a German beer-tastings session. "Now that sounds fun," he concluded.

And he still had an unconditional offer from Lancaster. Very different now from its status as one of the "new" universities when I graduated fifty summers ago. Very different, what's more, from an ancient public school in the prosperous Home Counties, then and now.

Still, this is a lad who had won a scholarship to Eton from Lordswood Boys' School in Birmingham. He was more than used to adapting to marked contrasts.

James Cheam-Smith, classical guitarist and Etonian

James with his parents, Julie and Glen

James in full Etonian regalia with his sister Jess

Decline and Fall to Rise and Shine

Chapter Five

New School Opens and Shuts

Invitations to parents and others to come and see for themselves the spacious, high-tech interior of Lordswood Boys' School mark two had been hastily withdrawn. The "grand opening" had been postponed until heaven knows when. This year, next year, some time. Nobody knew for sure. All we did know was that the virus known as Corona, or Covid-19, had arrived on these shores with a vengeance. We also knew that it wouldn't be leaving any time soon.

Those of us old enough to remember when Corona was a brand of pop with a distinctive top, delivered by the "Corona man" in his "Corona van", would shortly be expected to shut ourselves away for months on end. Meanwhile, the football season had been suspended while theatres and cinemas, pubs, clubs and restaurants were being closed down. It wouldn't be long before ever-more-stringent Government edicts would demand that schools follow suit.

Sure enough, the announcement came on Wednesday March 18. Two days previously I'd had a brief opportunity for a private tour around the new school, sited just behind the old building which was fenced off and awaiting demolition.

A lad assiduously rubbing his hands with some sanitising wipe pointed me towards the new front door where a familiar figure stood behind the reception desk. Jasbinder Thandi it was who had shown me around the old school. Today that role was to be taken on by the deputy head, Rajdip Kang, who would be with me shortly. For now Jas introduced me to her daughter, Simrun, who waved from the phone call that she was answering while helping out her Mum. On a temporary basis, mind you. "She's going to be a barrister," Jas mouthed proudly

When I had chance to chat to Simrun, she told me that she had three degrees. First there'd been a BSc in business and politics from Aston University, followed by a Masters in international relations and global governance. "Then I did a graduate diploma in law," she said. "I'm just waiting for my contract to arrive for a job at the Ministry of Justice. I'll start training for the Bar later this year."

At this point I remembered Jas telling me about her father. Jagpal Ratu had arrived in this country from the Punjab not too long after the British withdrawal from India and the carnage that had followed. He'd started in Bradford, working as a welder by day and crying himself to sleep at night while lying on the floor of a house occupied by many another seeking a new life in the "old country".

As a Bradford lad himself, Central Academies Trust chief executive David Kershaw had vivid childhood memories of those bad old days. His father, the man charged with collecting rates for the City Council, once took him to a property in inner-city Lumb Lane where "there must have been twenty or more young men" strewn across the floor, wrapped in rugs. "They were just getting up to make room for the next shift. I was five or six at the time and found it deeply upsetting."

So did "Dad", apparently. Kershaw senior duly made an official complaint to the local authority about the "inhuman exploitation by the mill owners".

Not that Jas's dad Jagpal hung around to find out what the outcome had been. Having heard that wages were better in the West Midlands than West Yorkshire, he moved to Smethwick and started work in a local foundry. "He did two men's jobs and raised the money to buy a house," Jas had told me. "Then he went back to India to marry my mother before bringing her back here," she added before going on to say, "A real grafter was my Dad."

So much so that he was still picking litter on the playground and playing fields of Lordswood Boys until he wasn't far off ninety. Quite a lot of litter, apparently, in the days before the CAT took over. "The place was quite a mess until Dad arrived," Jas remembered.

And now his granddaughter was on course to become a barrister, I mused, having noticed on the way in the fresh Tarmac of the new playground gleaming in the sun with not a discarded sweet wrapper to be seen. At this point the door opened and a beaming deputy head appeared.

Raj Kang turned out to be another example of someone from a family with its roots a long way from this country that had transformed its prospects within a generation or two. Her father had been a farmer back in the Punjab and started work in Birmingham as a milkman. Went on to build up a milk wholesale business, mind you, profitable enough for him to acquire a decent-sized family home in upmarket Sutton Coldfield.

And her mother?

"She's always been a housewife and speaks little English," Raj reflected. Punjabi has remained her native tongue. Yet all six of her children have been to university – Leicester to study bio-chemistry in Raj's case. "One of my brothers is a dentist, another's an optometrist." Sisters? "One's a medical rep and another's a teacher."

All three of her own children, incidentally, have been to King Edward's School in Edgbaston. Two are still there and one is now in his second year of a degree in medicine after notching up ten 'A' stars and another mere 'A' at GCSE, plus scoring forty-four out of forty-five in his International Baccalaureate.

Ms Kang, as I should call her (albeit "Miss" to any passing pupils) started teaching chemistry here at Lordswood Boys back in 2005 – the same year that Headteacher Lee Williams joined the art department. She'd soon be showing me around the new chemistry labs with professional pride. But first we adjourned to her office to chat about the ups and downs that she'd witnessed in her fifteen years here.

"A lot of changes in leadership," she mused. "Not to mention changes across the board in terms of staffing. We've seen results go right down and our numbers [of students] go right down."

Did she feel like packing up and moving on at any point?

"I don't think I did. I've always loved the feel of the school and what we're trying to achieve here. We have so many students who come from the Pupil Premium background." They're entitled to free school meals, in other words. Which begged the question of whether they'd get at least one nourishing meal a day during their prolonged absence from school.

At the time of our chat the closure of schools was still a few days away, so that thought hung in the air. It came down to earth when it was confirmed that supermarket vouchers would be sent out to those students, or packed lunches would be made available.

Sorry to interrupt, Ms Kang. How did you feel about the coming of the CAT in 2017?

"When the Trust came they were really transparent about what their vision was."

So much so that some of the messages were pinned to the noticeboard on the office wall behind her. About "knowing the vulnerabilities of all students"; about "identifying the right provision for all pupils"; about "monitoring and evaluation of impact." And so on.

And please go on, deputy head.

"A journey of school improvement can be quite long. It's not immediate. Intent, implementation and impact were the three things we had to focus on. And it's all about focus – we were going to do something, drive it well and see what the impact is."

So you've seen it work?

"Absolutely. I can't say that it's been easy. It's been a very difficult journey but the highlights have been great," she reflected before adding that literacy was the key driver on that journey.

"It's embedded through the staff and the way we teach. We have to make the students realise how important literacy is. They need it to access exam papers [though not in the summer of 2020, as it transpired]. It's also about being able to function in the workplace when they leave school, communicating well and building up their confidence through their reading and writing skills. You can stop the boys anywhere in the school and ask them 'what's your reading age and how much have you improved'? And they could all answer you with confidence."

At this point a hooter sounded loudly, signalling the end of the school day. Within another few days that hooter would signal the end of school before the end of March. And the vast majority of pupils wouldn't be back until September. What's more, community libraries would be closing down along with just about everything else. Year-seven organised trips to Thimblemill Library in Smethwick would have to be abandoned.

For the time being at least, the school library was still open upstairs. "A couple of years ago the library was very much a niche for the few," said Ms Kang as the noise from the hooter faded away. "Now it's a key part of what we do: the idea of reading for fun and enjoyment as well as attainment."

Time, perhaps, to go and have a look at the new library. And much else besides.

On the way we passed toilets that I was assured were well equipped with sanitisers as well as signage about the importance of washing hands. And there had been no reported cases at the school by the time the closure came. Assemblies had been devoted to the Coronavirus. Science lessons too.

I could tell that the former head of chemistry was dying to show me the abundance of laboratories with new equipment a-plenty. Not to mention running water – all too often an occasional option in the labs of old, I was told.

But as it happened, the music room came into view first. Or should I say rooms? Far less cluttered than I remembered from my old-school tour with Jas. Keyboards galore were ranged around expansive walls. Plenty of drum kits as well. "They've got four rehearsal rooms, including a guitar studio," the deputy head confided before we were re-joined by music teacher Marie Lowndes-Ford who had been about to take a group of year-seven pupils to see the CBSO at the Symphony Hall last time we'd met.

As we were re-introduced, I noticed a saxophone gleaming among other instruments in a glass display case. "It's rather an old sax and beyond repair," said Ms L-F. "But we're planning to start a project about brass instruments. Somebody's coming in from the Education Department to give them free lessons for the rest of the year."

"Might get some jazz players out of it," I suggested.

"Well, you never know."

What we do know now but didn't know at the time was that the school would soon be closed for the rest of the term. And beyond. Brass "ed" off?

Afraid so.

For now at least there was so much optimism in the air as we passed a five-a-side football match in full flow beneath many a basketball hoop in a huge sports hall. I sensed a quickening of the Kang step as up the stairs we bounded to her beloved Science Department, now with all mod cons.

There were fume cupboards "for practicals". A huge screen dominated one wall. Not just any old screen but an "interactive screen".

Gleaming taps offered gushing hot and cold water at any time. "And this is the prep room with lots of equipment," the deputy head enthused.

Chemistry lessons in my day seemed to evolve around Bunsen burners and blackboards chalked with unfathomable formulae. Not that I took much notice. As the "master" droned on, I was mentally engaged elsewhere, picking world cricket and football XIs to take part in inter-planetary matches at some future date – or dreaming about girls as the years advanced interminably. I was rewarded with a grade nine at what was then chemistry GCE. No, that wasn't a top grade. It was bottom of the pile in a system in which a grade one was as good as you could get. And, no, I wasn't that much better at biology and physics.

But I tried to look knowledgeable as Raj, as I could surely refer to her now that most students had gone home, showed me rock cycles, skeletons and an oscilloscope. "Ah, yes, of course," I muttered before she went on to point out that "every room in the department has a library packed with books".

And talking of books, we would soon be at the library, once we'd gazed out of high windows at expansive playing fields and tennis courts one way and down at a deserted canteen the other. Six padded stools in royal blue were ranged along ten lengthy tables. All empty and now, it would seem, likely to remain that way for the foreseeable future.

Rows of raised seating in matching blue will remain empty too in the auditorium where assemblies were due to be held twice a week. Not religious assemblies, needless to say – too many differing creeds. So apart from the threat of the virus and the necessary precautions, what might the subjects be?

"One might be about attendance and the importance of being in school. Another might be about the importance of literacy." Raj paused before adding that "we have students delivering assemblies as well. It boosts their confidence. The year-sevens love it."

But they're only eleven or twelve. What do they talk about?

"They read from their books or share book reviews."

And do the older ones sit there and listen politely?

"On World Book Day we had ten readers. Some of them were EAL students [English as an Additional Language] and obviously they weren't particularly fluent. But they were listened to attentively and with respect. And I think the respect was for the fact that someone had the confidence to stand there and do it."

Books seemed to be everywhere. Classroom walls were lined with shelves. In one, quite possibly the English Room, I noticed *Othello* and *The Tempest*, Hardy's *Mayor of Casterbridge*, Dickens's *Bleak House* and many more. There also were quotes from authors on doors. Maya Angelou here, Roald Dahl there.

If memory serves, Dahl was on the door of the library itself. Plenty more books here, needless to say, and computer screens were ranged all along the far side of the room. Every one of them was occupied. "These are year-eleven students who need access to resources," Raj whispered. "They're studying for their exams."

As it transpired, the exams were soon to be suspended. Indefinitely. GCSE grades would be awarded largely according to progress students had made in the school year, evidenced by school data. And classwork would have to continue on websites such as Google Classroom, often in cramped properties in parts of the city where conditions were hardly conducive to quiet studying. Meanwhile, "access to resources" provided by libraries would be closed off.

Only thirteen students, the sons of key workers in the NHS and elsewhere, would be allowed to continue attending this inspirational new building that had cost the Department for Education some fourteen and a half million – money that may not have been forthcoming were it not for the Trust's transformation of Lordswood Boys.

One day it would reopen. But at that stage nobody knew exactly when. The closure of schools was necessary, of course, to stem the spread of a virus that had the potential to cripple our much treasured National Health Service and provide a widespread harvest for the Grim Reaper.

Necessary but frustrating: for the staff, for the students and for members of the Trust that had done so much to change attitudes and achievements.

The most active, hands-on member of CAT is Director of School Improvement Michael Rennie and we'll be finding out a bit more about his background, motives and methods in the next chapter. For now he gave me a brief, emailed response to the close-down:

"It's desperate for all students, but especially for year elevens. They were in line to break all school achievements and would have done exceptionally well – something of a norm for LBS these days.

"It's a double blow, having only just moved to the new school, but it is what it is. Everyone is in this and it's beyond words, obviously. Connecting with our students is tricky but in this age of connectivity, it is amazing what can be done. Our staff have been great in supplying work for our students and it is a strong response, all things considered."

New dining area, devoid of diners

New assembly area, devoid of assemblies

Chapter Six

The Two Rennies

Michael Rennie is the man at the sharp end – the one who knows that you don't improve a school that has been in special measures without making fundamental changes. And you don't make changes without upsetting those who were failing. "I'm perceived by some as perhaps a bit edgy," confided the Director of School Improvement. "But basically I like walking my dogs, having a good red wine and watching football. I'm not heavily into social media or doing political things behind the scenes. I just want to get the job done."

That was a quote from our second meeting, in a café just down the road from where he lives in Earlsdon, Coventry. We were enjoying a pre-Corona coffee. The virus had yet to close down cafés and just about everything else, including schools. Mind you, its dire threat was looming over the horizon and had already led to the temporary cancellation of the new Lordswood Boys' School's official opening for parents, local dignitaries and others.

The closure of the school to all but a handful of Lordswood boys would follow soon after. But, like the café, it was still open at the time we met.

Michael's mood seemed a somewhat brighter than it had been at our previous meeting. He was also sporting a distinctively bright check jacket as well as a grey hat decorated with metal badges. They included anything from memorabilia of the First World War, a subject with which he has a personal fascination, to insignia of Manchester City, a club to which he has had a lifetime's dedication.

His sartorial flamboyance confirmed my suspicion that this was a man with a distinctive style and self-belief. Bit of a maverick perhaps and never quite predictable.

Despite having had to delay the "grand opening", he seemed decidedly enthusiastic about the new school at Lordswood. "It's fantastic, off the scale. We can't fail in that building. It's large and spacious. And every classroom is climate controlled with very good acoustics."

We'd been introduced previously in his office at the old school where the walls had borne evidence of one of his great passions: football. Pictures of the New York Yankees featured almost as prominently as Manchester City.

On that occasion he was wearing a blue shirt with a white collar. A colourful handkerchief spilled from the breast pocket of his striped jacket. But his mood had seemed surprisingly downbeat. His frustration at not being able to apply his transformational formula to other schools was almost palpable.

He'd very briefly been Headteacher at Lordswood Boys in 2016, but the role was not right for him at that time and other ideas were dominating his mind-set. Based on past successes, he felt strongly that there was a definite pathway for Lordswood, a route out of the nadir. The outcomes in 2017, when the new Trust came in, were the lowest in the history of the school. Something had to change. And quickly.

Wasn't there an understanding at that time between teachers and students?

"That was my phrase: 'the Lordswood deal'. It amounted to 'We won't push you too hard if you don't give us hassle'. It's one of half a dozen characteristics of failing schools, wherever you go. Some people do not take responsibility. They're often trying to pass it on to someone else: a culture of referral, in a sense. Courage was lacking in all facets of the school and it showed. So over our first year here we held up the mirror and encouraged people to reflect on past practice, challenging them to change and improve."

One who did not lack courage was his daughter Clare whom we'll be meeting in the next chapter. In fact, she just came in to help out – stood out too as a born teacher, despite having no professional qualifications in that field. He must have been disappointed, I'd suggested, that she'd chosen a career in the courtroom rather than the classroom.

"No. I wouldn't advise anybody to go into education. It's somewhat broken," he shrugged.

Surely this place (Lordswood) proved exactly the opposite?

"What happens here doesn't mean that the system is fine. But your constituency of students here is what keeps you going. They're the most worthy in my view because they've got the hardest life to come in front of them as the vast majority are not white. Particularly in this country as we lurch ever more rightwards politically."

"You sound very disillusioned," I said, pointing out the bleeding obvious, before going on, "You must be pleased that this school has turned round in such a short time."

"Yes, but where are the other projects? It's been truly transformative for the students here and could have positive, generational changes and effects on their families going forward. But where are the additional schools that we thought our Trust would be getting so that we could apply this model to them? Arguably, this is the most transformational model for schools anywhere on the planet. So powerful and so well thought through. And, what is more, it's tried and tested.

"What we did in Coventry has been applied here but much more quickly in a more refined, considered and strategic fashion. But it is essentially the same model based on leadership, accountability, better teaching, better recruitment and simple, understandable solutions consistently and relentlessly applied. It's about delivering a plan, 'getting it done' as the Americans say.

"This necessitates having an integrated planning approach where you use your budget well to ensure the recruitment of high quality teachers, retain them and pay them properly. You have to balance the budget by spending on the things that matter, simplify the curriculum and recruit for the next phase in a timely fashion. Then develop your yardsticks, real-time metrics to inform progress.

"More powerful than perhaps anything else is our development of and continuous commitment to literacy. In 2017 we measured the reading ages of all our students and found that across the school, on average, students were forty-four months behind chronological age. By year-eleven, the 'Literacy Gap' had grown to fifty-eight months, almost five years adrift. And which exams were they going to pass with that level of reading ability? How can students' reading ability actually decline over the five years that they're in school? We have implemented and continue to develop and refine a whole-school literacy strategy, brilliantly led by our Deputy Head Raj Kang. As a result, the literacy gap across the school has been reduced by seventy-nine per cent. And if their reading improvement continues at the current trajectory, we project that by the exam season of 2022 the year-eleven students will have no gap at all, on average.

"That model is so powerful. So why, having had three years of stellar change at Lordswood, aren't the Government saying to us, 'How did you do that? Have a go at this school; have a go at that one.' I totally believe in what I'm doing and have the track record to prove it. So what is it that's stopping us from spreading it wider?"

(Our first meeting had been in that period that might be called BC: Before Corona. The virus had since been spreading itself wider through the UK. Accordingly, Government thinking and expenditure had been targeted almost exclusively on health rather than education or just about anything else.)

At least the mood of the chief improvement officer had lifted a bit when I mentioned David Kershaw, a friend of the Rennie family since Michael's childhood. "David empowers me," he acknowledged. "The improvement strategy of the school is my job and David is a really good sounding board for this. I don't think we've disagreed on anything. We just have this very close understanding. But for him I wouldn't still be doing this. I'd have walked away ages ago as I was so very disillusioned with education and what I could see coming down the pipeline."

Michael Rennie was born in Manchester fifty-five years ago but was sent to Coventry aged six. Well, the city was considered a pioneer of comprehensive education at the time. And his father, John Rennie, was appointed chief adviser to the local council's education department and was familiar with David Kershaw's work in transforming low-performing Coundon Court into arguably the best state school in town. Didn't always see eye to eye, apparently, but then one was a Yorkshireman and the other a Lancastrian. Both would have had trenchant opinions on the way forward, one imagines.

Certainly John Rennie was none too happy when his son turned down the chance of going to the prestigious Goldsmiths College, part of the University of London, in order to go to Manchester Polytechnic. "Absolutely furious," according to Michael, who went on to admit that "yes, it was a stupid thing to do".

So why do it?

"I knew that I just wanted to be closer to the City and I have always cast myself as a professional Mancunian".

That would be Manchester City, needless to say. He went on to say, "I had a season ticket for Maine Road [City's former ground] and the opportunity to live in the shadow of the grand old stadium and to walk there on a Saturday was too much of a pull. Crazy really. Ironically, the year I went to poly was the year they were relegated. It was 1983 and Luton Town scored in the last minute to put us down. Yes, I was there".

Nearly forty years on and much has changed, in football and in education. But it could be argued that the Rennies have been dedicated to scoring equalisers on behalf of those at the bottom of the table(s). Making a difference to children's chances seems to run in the family. Michael had just received new data that very morning of our second meeting which suggested that the Lordswood Boys' pass level at GCSE was likely to be over eighty per cent in English and maths "for the first time in the school's history". (Stop press: eighty-eight per cent and eighty-two per cent respectively, confirmed 2020 outcomes.)

Not that they would be sitting exams, as it transpired, in the plagued summer of 2020. But the data was as always highly accurate, student progress being among the key metrics that are pursued almost on a daily basis.

It seemed set to become one of the best non-grammar schools in Birmingham, I suggested.

"For sure," he confirmed before going on to answer my subsequent question about the King Edwards grammar schools in Birmingham and beyond. Didn't he find their "creaming off" of the brightest children frustrating – especially so as the son of champion of comprehensive education and indeed a pioneer of community education? Not for the first time, Michael Rennie confounded my expectations.

"Well, the longest time I ever spent teaching in one school was at King Edward's in Stratford-upon-Avon," he reflected. "I worked there for nearly nine years. Invigilating exams in a room where Shakespeare was apparently educated was pretty special. And a lot of our sixth-formers went on to Oxbridge.

"Admittedly my father didn't speak to me for a year after I took up that job." Despite, it would seem, the senior Rennie having been to North Manchester Grammar School while his son was a product of one of his beloved Coventry comprehensives.

"But, Michael went on, "KES Stratford was where I learnt my craft. I learnt how to teach so that I knew what I was talking about, in a sense serving a long apprenticeship of classroom teaching. My subjects were economics and maths and I had just one promotion when I became

Head of Economics. Too many graduates come into the profession now and push for promotion when they're not remotely experienced enough, climbing the salary scale as fast as they can. I understand the economics of that but in reality many build their careers on feet of clay."

At this point the former Head of Economics began to talk about "high equity". Thankfully, he went on to explain its relevance to education.

"I've done training with whole rooms full of teachers and I say to them, 'What's your motivation for being a teacher?' They'll talk about great holidays, good pension, a steady job, a love of young people, wanting to make a contribution and other similar worthy reasons. And I say, 'Does anyone think about high equity?'"

Many times this leads to blank faces all round.

"Then I have to explain," Michael explained, "that I think education is a great equaliser. It's the way out at the time when you have sixty percent of kids living in poverty. That's true of an even higher percentage in our school. Get those grades and it can change their lives. It means that their own kids will be different. The cycle of poverty is broken. To me that's high equity and that's the reason to do this job. Schools are community locomotives, powerful engines of change – a lasting, sustainable change that can, if done well, impact the well-being of communities for generations. If done badly, the impact of the inevitable damage can be just as profound.

"My long-term vision for that school [Lordswood] is for it to be essentially a grammar school available to the poorest boys in Birmingham. And we're getting there bit by bit. Those boys have to have the aspiration to go to university. There's been a horrible attitude towards immigration in this country over the past few years but I contend that some of the most aspirational people that we have in our society are from the immigrant community. It really matters to them to get on. They often have additional pressures such as language barriers and cultural isolation but they came here for very good reasons, sometimes in desperation. I see them as people we should help and support, and education is one of the keys."

The lack of a sixth-form at Lordswood Boys' had been another source of frustration to him, as I recalled from our previous meeting. But that could change as its results keep rising and the Rennie dream of a "grammar school for poorest" comes closer.

After leaving King Edward's Grammar School in Stratford, Michael had moved to a very different school in a very different world, all of twenty miles away. Woodway Park (now the Grace Academy) was in the throes of Special Measures and was at the time the school in that category longer than any other school in England and Wales.

Wood End, Coventry, was the location – a place I remember all too well as a deprived former council estate where I'd reported on street riots for *The Observer* in 1992. Wood End harboured a misnamed pub called the Live and Let Live where I'd found myself standing ankle deep in broken glass interviewing an amiable local while petrol bombs lit up the night sky around us.

Time to get back to school, perhaps. Sorry, Michael, you were saying:

"Very few people would have gone from a grammar school (and one with such a prestigious reputation) sector to Woodway Park, but I felt that I had some ideas to pass on, something valuable, perhaps some sort of mark to make."

His title was "Inclusion Manager" and, in that capacity, he originated an "Alternative Curriculum" for disaffected students as well as a "discrete support and skills facility" for younger ones showing signs of disaffection. What's more, he initiated a new approach to SEN provision – help with the move from primary to secondary education, in other words. Not forgetting his implementation of a reading programme for Key Stage 3, covering the first three years at secondary school.

Woodway Park came out of Special Measures and Ofsted's report made mention of the Rennie initiatives as a strength of the school. Result: not just one but two invitations to Number 10, Downing Street. On the second occasion he was introduced to no less a figure than Sir Michael Barber, head of Tony Blair's Delivery Unit on literacy and unity. "Interesting times," Michael reflected, "though little came of those visits."

Still, I suspect that his father might have been rather proud of his work at Woodway Park and, indeed, his recognition in high places. After all, John Rennie had built up quite a reputation in the world of education. And not just in the UK.

"Dad managed to get funding from the Manpower Services Commission for the community education project in Coventry," his son recalled. "There were nineteen or twenty schools taking part in what was almost a national experiment in the 1970s. Then it became a worldwide thing. In a sense, the world of community education came to our house when we were kids. We'd sit there listening to Professor So-and-so from the University of Columbia holding forth. Other esteemed professionals from every corner of the education world came as well, from Australia, Brazil and Germany. They were really interesting people with amazing information about education," he added before seeing off his Americano.

By now I'd long ago finished my espresso. Time to move on, perhaps. After all, the Rennie "sounding board" was due to arrive soon. Every week Michael had a meeting with David Kershaw to discuss Lordswood issues here in the café some twenty five miles or so from Harborne. Mind you, that was BC: before Corona and before closure. It wouldn't be long before meetings had to be conducted via Zoom, Skype, email or even British Telecom.

It was through mobile phone that I sought a bit more insight into the inspirational character that had been John Rennie. I'd vaguely remembered the name from the Kershaw autobiography that I'd ghost-written. "Hadn't he been a visiting lecturer when you were a mature student at Nottingham University in the early 1970s?" I asked David when we finally connected.

Yes, was the short answer to that. And, yes, it was John Rennie who had persuaded young Kershaw, all of five years his junior, to move to the educational Shangri-la that Coventry was seen as in those days. At least for those seeking a more egalitarian system. The city "leading the way in eliminating the divisions put between children at the age of eleven by the grammar-and-secondary-modern system", to quote from the book.

Now to quote David from our more recent mobile phone conversation, "John was grindingly committed not only to comprehensive education but to community education for people of all ages. At Coundon Court, adults would join our A-level classes. They could be in their thirties, forties, fifties or sixties, and they had a lot to offer. At the same time it was a chance for them to see young people in a different light. Not as hooligans but as diligent and inquisitive students. It was John who encouraged heads to develop those wider relationships."

And not just in school, it would seem. John Rennie also encouraged teachers to hold meetings in what were then called "working men's clubs" on council estates such as Canley, where David had become deputy head at the local comprehensive in the early 1970s. Men who had left school as early as possible to earn a decent living in car factories were – eventually – introduced to issues such as local history. They would also be encouraged to spend some of their spare time reading with their children. And after a while women were invited to join the groups. Had to be signed in, mind you, and wouldn't be allowed anywhere near such hallowed male-only sanctuaries as the snooker room.

"John was the driving force behind those initiatives, a real agent of change," David recalled. "As a result, he made a lot of friends but also quite a few enemies. He was an interesting, flamboyant character and what you might call reasonably impatient. Told people what he thought."

Which sounded familiar, I suggested.

"Oh yes. Michael has inherited so many characteristics of his father."

And Clare Rennie, it seemed, had inherited her father's teaching talents and the ability to convey the demands of the curriculum to a classroom packed with unlikely students of the works of Wordsworth, Blake and Shelley.

How?

We're about to find out.

Michael Rennie, a major transformative figure

Chapter Seven

From Classroom to Courtroom

Question one: Is Lionel Messi the greatest footballer of all time? Discuss.

But not here if you don't mind.

Question two: Would Clare Rennie have been a great teacher?

No discussion required.

She dazzled during an all too brief appearance at Lordswood Boys School – hence her nickname as "the Lionel Messi of the classroom". Given to her by her father, as it happened.

"Ridiculously," she smiled.

Still, as the last chapter made plain, Michael Rennie can be quite demanding when it comes to teaching standards. The Director of School Improvement at Lordswood Boys is not one to lavish praise where it's not been earned. He's also a man with a passion for football as well as improving the chances of children and teenagers written off as no-hopers in the league table of life.

Clare had just turned twenty-five when we met in the same Coventry café where I'd interviewed him, albeit on a different day. Well, she does still live a few hundred yards away, at the home of her parents, while studying in Birmingham for a graduate diploma in law.

A diminutive figure in size but not in personality, she would have been just twenty-three during her fleeting virtuoso performance in the Lordswood classroom. And younger still when she'd made her debut at Ash Green, on the northern borders of Coventry, in the days when "Dad" was deputy head.

"I was in my gap year between A-levels and university," she recalled. "Luckily the school had a very efficient head of English. I learnt a lot from her and quickly realised that it was all about being prepared for the lesson ahead."

Still, it must have been quite daunting to walk into a Lordswood classroom full of boisterous boys, most of whom would have towered over her, and try to engage them in the works of Tennyson and Shelley. Apart from anything else, English was a second language to some of those lads. Tennyson's *Charge of the Light Brigade*? She must have felt as though there were cannons to the right of her and cannons to the left.

"It was easy," she breezed. "No issue. I'd been warned that they were going to be really difficult. But if you treat them with respect then they treat you with respect."

By the time of her Lordswood debut, she already had a degree in English Literature from Nottingham University. Now all she had to do was get a lot of fifteen and sixteen-year-old boys ready for their GCSE exams while being aware that many of them had "reading ages three years or more behind their chronological ages".

Easy?

"The way I built a bond with them was through football," she recalled. "I'd watched them in the playground and quickly realised that very few of them supported the local Birmingham teams."

"Not even the Villa," I sighed to myself as a one-time stalwart of the Holte End.

"They were all for the top sides, particularly Liverpool," Clare went on. "But that was the season when City dominated."

Manchester City, needless to say. Not Coventry City and certainly not Birmingham City. A talent for teaching was hardly the only thing she'd inherited from her father.

"I had endless fun just ribbing those boys," she went on. "When you're teaching something like Macbeth, you could find allegories within the text. I'd always present Liverpool as the main character, doing anything they could for power. But it was Macduff who ended up reigning supreme for City."

She paused to check something on her laptop before going on to say, "I'd been aware from the start that a lot of them were disengaged. It wasn't that they didn't want to do well; it was that they didn't want to appear to do well."

Was that because they felt the need to look "cool" in front of their classmates?

"No, it was because they had absolutely no confidence in their own abilities and so were afraid to sound stupid when they made comments about their interpretation of the works. Once they gained their confidence and felt better about themselves, they would perform and sometimes say things that surpassed any of my expectations."

Apart from works by Tennyson and Shelley, Robert Browning and William Wordsworth, the GCSE syllabus included poets of more recent vintage, including Seamus Heaney, Ted Hughes and Simon Armitage. Not forgetting two Carols – Carol Ann Duffy and Carol Rumens. Nonetheless, Clare was conscious that some of the boys might find the curriculum "outdated". And she wasn't afraid to tell them that.

Nor did she shy away from showing them that what they were learning was also relevant; that "everything they would see in life would, in some way, relate to what they were learning there". And that "they were going to have to learn an anthology of poems, go into the exam and be able to regurgitate everything they knew about them".

To explain that relevance and build some confidence, she started with an American rap artist. No, Kanye West was not on the curriculum. He is, however, renowned for his lyrics. "I picked a song that was full of metaphor," Clare recalled, "and challenged them to discuss what he was actually talking about. It was a work of poetry."

After that she had them "eating out of her hand", as David Kershaw had told me before going on to say with head-shaking regret, "She was a natural."

A natural teacher, needless to say. Runs in the Rennie family all too evidently, along with a strong belief in social justice. But, like her father, I suspect that Clare is not one to be easily pinned down and categorised.

"The whole point of doing the year at Lordswood was to be able to afford my graduate diploma," she told me. "I'd already done a law conversion degree after English Lit at Nottingham. Now I'm training to be a barrister. And I want to work in crime.

"At Lordswood I could see that quite a few of the boys were influenced by gangs. Luckily that didn't make its way into the school, but I could tell that there were issues on the outside. A couple of the boys did run into some difficulties while I was there, and I saw how horribly unnavigable the system is. I saw myself defending people like them but also prosecuting the grooming gangs."

And once she had the necessary qualification she'd be happy to do that anywhere in the country. "But preferably in Birmingham," she smiled. "It has my heart. God knows why. I think it's having been a teacher at the school. Since then I've had a real feeling of warmth towards the city. Mind you, that divide between Harborne on one side of the Hagley Road and Bearwood on the other sums up everything about society at the moment."

The school, as we know, is on the Harborne side. Its students come from the other side – "of the tracks" if not the Hagley Road itself. Clare has been aware of that ever since her time as a teacher there.

"It was the most fulfilling year of my life," she admitted. "Ever since it has been the driving force for everything that I want to do. I could see that there were so many significant factors in their lives beyond the classroom. And those other things out there are what I want to get them out of."

One boy, she recalled, had been arrested on a charge of armed robbery just before his English literature GCSE. "He didn't even take the exam. And he was a student who should have exceeded his target grades," she added before going on to say that "six hours a day at school is not always enough to change a cycle of poverty".

And since our conversation the Coronavirus had ensured that the vast majority of Lordswood boys wouldn't be allowed one hour, let alone six, in school and away from homes on the mean streets of inner-city Birmingham and Bearwood. Yes, they could still learn on-line. But that's not always easy in overcrowded accommodation with distractions all around, as Clare would have been well aware.

She would also be aware that should her aspirations to defend the innocent and condemn the guilty end in disillusion with the legal system, there would always be a job for her in the education sector.

Schools would be open again one day. But, for the time being, nobody knew just when.

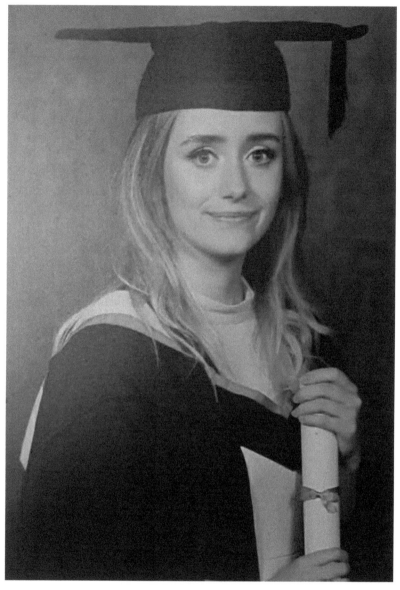

*The Lionel Messi of the classroom on her graduation
from Nottingham University*

Chapter Eight

The Long Lockdown

As it transpired, school resumed in early June – but only for some children in some infants and junior classes. Even that was an issue of contention. Teachers' unions had their concerns about enforcing social distancing. Many parents were also worried. Although death rates were falling, the virus was far from under control. How were schools going to keep their "little 'uns" two metres apart at all times?

Most of their older brothers and sisters at senior schools such as Lordswood Boys wouldn't be returning until September at the earliest. By which time they would have been away from their classrooms for the best part of six months. The exceptions were students in year-ten who were allowed back in mid-June [see Chapter Nine]. After all, they were approaching their final year at the school.

GCSEs loomed. And working from home was hardly ideal for those, like many a Lordswood lad, living in cramped conditions with large families. A report by the Institute for Fiscal Studies, released in mid-May, confirmed what most of us suspected – that the attainment gap between pupils from poor and comparatively wealthy families had widened during the lockdown.

For much of that seemingly interminable time adolescents bursting with hormonal energy would be expected to stay at home and get their heads down. Or rather keep their chins up and their eyes on screens conveying the likes of Google Classroom, BBC Bitesize and more.

Staff at Lordswood had been doing their best to help. Assistant head Jane Thompson, otherwise known as the "safeguarding lead", had been making regular visits to some of the families most in need of support. So had the school's designated educational social worker. And neither had stepped inside, needless to say. They'd kept their distance on the doorstep.

Regular parcels from the school's food bank had also been dropped off. Tucker galore had been donated by staff, topping up the deliveries deemed necessary for those entitled to free school meals. What's more, laptops and tablets had been forthcoming for those families where such expensive gadgets had been in short supply.

One of them was for Jason Griffiths (not his real name) who had spent four months living in temporary accommodation with his mother and five siblings when I finally had a chance to chat to him. By that time he had been let back into school thanks to the efforts of another assistant head, Lindsay Greatrix, whose specialist subject is German.

"We'd had a call from Social Services and Jane passed the case on to me as I'd taught his elder brother," she explained. "The family had been living in very limited accommodation in Ladywood and were due to move into a new place. That was delayed by Covid-19, so the local authority moved them into two rooms in a small hotel on the Hagley Road. Jason didn't have access to a computer or even a laptop. I'd take work packs round at regular intervals – paper copies, along with some books from our library.

"Mum had told me that he'd become very frustrated. But he was reluctant to come back to school at first because he didn't think there'd be anybody else there. In fact, it has made so much difference to him. He did a lot of work on the first day and left with a big smile on his face."

When I finally met Jason, he'd been back in school for three weeks. He's twelve years old and of mixed race. His mother had been a hotel cleaner – although not at the hotel where she's now confined with her family. "Dad" lives elsewhere and works "in construction and that".

Or so Jason told me after I'd asked him what it was like to be back in year-eight at Lordswood, alongside a few sons of key workers. "It's made a big difference to me," he confirmed. "I really couldn't get much done where we're staying. There are computers and stuff here."

What were you doing all day at the hotel?

"I was on my phone a lot. Then it broke and I had to borrow my sister's now and again."

He has two sisters older than him, one of whom is seventeen and pregnant, as well as two twin younger sisters, aged four. Sleeping arrangements at their temporary accommodation have been complicated to say the least.

"There have been a lot of you in just two rooms," I suggested, pointing out the obvious.

"Yeah. It was driving me mad when I couldn't go any further than the garden."

He looked understandably sad at that point. Then he cheered up when he pointed out that one of his mates was among the few boys working silently and diligently in the classroom next door. Jason's favourite subject is art and that's what he was evidently itching to return to.

"I keep trying to get him to do a bit more German," said Lindsay wistfully as Jason bade us farewell and headed back to his computer with a spring in his step. Ironically, perhaps, he wanted to make the most of his comparative freedom before the school holidays loomed.

Meanwhile, Michael Rennie had, of necessity, become a remote Director of School Improvement, working on-line. Apart from anything else, he'd spent up to six hours a day linked to five other members of staff in order to "come up with an academically rigorous and exciting curriculum for year-seven pupils". Or so I was told by his "sounding board" David Kershaw.

David had seen some of the resources for history and geography lessons that they'd discovered on YouTube. "It's very high quality," he assured me. Quality work was coming back from the students, too, in many cases – "through Zoom, telephone calls or even the post".

There was a pause. "Still," he went on, "we know that these boys are missing the self-discipline of being in school. They need routine, rigour and support. Our other great frustration is that we have a wonderful new building and most of us aren't allowed in."

When I finally managed to catch the redoubtable Rennie on his mobile, his own understandable frustration was offset by some welcome developments. "We've managed to recruit twelve new teachers on Zoom," he revealed. "That means that we're fully staffed at last."

Fully funded as well, it would seem. "We've stabilised the budget after inheriting a deficit, and now have a bit of a surplus," he added.

Meanwhile, GCSE "results" had been submitted to the Department for Education sometime in mid-May. Not exam results, needless to say. There wouldn't be any exams in the summer of 2020. Grades would be decided on the basis of coursework and mock exams taken earlier in the year as a rehearsal for the real thing.

On that basis, the Lordswood lads had more than lived up to expectations. Some eighty-eight per cent had achieved the minimum pass mark of grade four in English. And eighty-two per cent had done the same in maths. The average for those two key subjects combined was a pass mark of seventy-eight per cent.

"That's the highest in my career," Michael confided with understandable pride. "It's two per cent higher than we achieved at Ash Green when we were flying. And it's way above the national average."

Not one of those boys, however, had been through what might be called the "real thing" as opposed to the mocks. They hadn't spent early summer's days sat in one of a line of desks, conscious of time ticking away while grappling with questions prescribed by official examining boards.

And those boards, it seemed, were sceptical. According to a story published in the i newspaper on June 19, "millions of proposed GCSE and A-levels could be downgraded by exam boards this summer because teachers have been too generous in their predictions".

Needless to say, those "millions" were all over the country, not just at Lordswood Boys in Birmingham. But it couldn't be taken for granted that the marks awarded in May would stand come "results day" in August.

We'd see.

Life can be cruel. Those year-elevens had been given the chance of a brave new world through the intervention of the Central Academies Trust. Now they wouldn't be going back to Lordswood as students. No sixth-form, remember. Not yet anyway. They would have to look elsewhere.

Just thirteen students, sons of key workers, were being educated at that "wonderful new building" that deputy head Rajdip Kang had showed me round just after it opened and shortly before it shut on March 20. [see Chapter Five].

During the months that followed, Raj and Headteacher Lee Williams made up the full-time staff. Each had three children of their own at home, which did little to ease the strain at the end of the school day. Other teachers were on a rota that called them in to the school not much more than once a fortnight. Working from home for the most part, they were setting and marking work through the Lordswood programme on the Google Classroom site.

"Staff had also been working closely on-line to formulate a best plan or a 'new-normal' for when schools are eventually allowed to reopen," Lee told myself and anything up to eleven million viewers on the education section of the Sikh Channel.

Yes, *eleven million*. Watched by Sikhs in many countries, in Punjabi and English, apparently. That's what Raj told me anyway after I'd seen an extract on YouTube.

When I finally located the "skip ad" logo, Raj herself looked slim and demure in a headscarf known as a "chunni". She's fluent in Punjabi, her mother having spoken little else when she grew up in Sutton Coldfield. Now here she was chatting with a be-turbaned interviewer before they switched to English and brought Lee into the conversation.

"Keep Calm and Carry On" was the essence of his message. "This isn't a time for panic. It's a time for us to be calm, supportive and put the children's safety first," he proclaimed to the camera.

Next question: "What can they expect when they finally come back to school?"

"Parents will need to know that schools are safe with social distancing in place. That's going to have to be supervised, even at break-time." There was also going to have to be a lot of cleaning and sanitising going on at regular intervals, he assured the interviewer.

He'd already assured me, on-line and on-phone, that no Lordswood boys had gone down with Covid-19. So far. "We are aware, though, that some elderly relatives of certain students have unfortunately contracted the virus."

Was he worried about the effects of this devastating virus on the Trust's transformation of Lordswood Boys from one of the worst to one of the best non-grammar schools in Birmingham?

No, was the short answer to that. "Because we know that the practices and principles that we've established here will be something they can step straight back into."

But that "step" back into Lordswood would be tentative and have to be several steps away from other pupils and staff members. Eventually, that is. For now the resumption of school seemed like a distant dream on a far horizon.

Chapter Nine

A Glimpse Through the Lockdown Keyhole

The report was critical, to put it mildly. One word summed up its conclusion: "inadequate". Quality of teaching, learning and assessment: "inadequate". Outcomes for pupils: "inadequate". Overall effectiveness: "inadequate". And so on.

The authors were inspectors from Ofsted, otherwise known as the Office for Standards in Education. The subject of the report was Lordswood Boys' School. The date of the inspection was October 4 and 5, 2016.

As we know, things have changed a bit since then.

Another inspection was due in the summer term of 2020. But that just happened to be a time when visits to places near and far were suspended. There wouldn't have been much for Ofsted inspectors to inspect, even if they had been allowed to come to Brum. Schools here and elsewhere were closed, for the most part.

Ofsted's absence was just one more setback for those who had worked so hard to transform Lordswood. "There are elements of frustration, yeah," Headteacher Lee Williams confirmed. "To be honest, an inspection would have allowed us to move the school on even further."

Not least by attracting more students, despite the additional complexities that may have added to the maintenance of social distancing come September. Who knows? More parents on this, the Harborne side of the Hagley Road, might have considered sending their sons here after reading what would surely have been a glowing report.

As for the social distancing issue, two areas were causing the most pressing concern. One was sport -- this at a time when the playing fields behind the new school seemed almost to be begging for someone to come and play on them.

The other area of concern was music. After all, it involves regular touching of instruments by one class after another. Blowing into them, too, in some cases. Suddenly it seemed a very long time ago since March when Marie Lowndes-Ford had proudly showed me around her new department with four rehearsal rooms and a guitar studio.

As for the damning inspection of 2016, that must seem like an eternity ago to those staff members and students who had been aroud at the time. Sukhra Kang, now fifteen, had arrived for his first year at Lordswood a month or so before the Ofsted inspection. "There was a new teacher every couple of months," he recalled.

A bit chaotic then?

"Oh yes."

And now?

"The teaching is consistently good."

Sukhra confirmed what I expected, but with the smile of someone who'd just enjoyed a brief return to something approaching normality. He was one of the year-ten students who'd been allowed back in to school for all of two hours a day.

It was just after eleven am when they'd emerged from a side door of the "new" school, laughing, joking and evidently enjoying what the Irish would have called the "craic" of being back together. Not for much longer, however. Their school day was over. For today anyway.

"Have a good afternoon, lads," called out the head, casually clad in shorts and short-sleeved shirt. Well, it was a gloriously hot, late-June day and he was about to send himself to Coventry. He had a meeting there with his Messrs Rennie and Kershaw in David Kershaw's garden, close to the great swathes of Shakespeare's Forest of Arden that still line both sides of the nearby road to Kenilworth. Deputy head Raj Kang would be there as well.

As for Sukhra, he'd soon be heading back to another Kang family home near Edgbaston Reservoir. He is of Indian heritage, although his father was born in England and works as a bus driver.

His Indian-born mother is a lunchtime supervisor at a school close to the family home. "She's out for not much more than an hour a day," Sukhra told me. "I've got an older sister and two younger brothers and we've all been a bit bored. In my case the school has been very good at setting work on-line, but once that's done I've missed going to the park with my mates. We haven't been much further than the back garden until now."

Now the lockdown was beginning to ease. Shops were opening for non-essential goods. Pubs and restaurants would pull back the rusting bolts on their doors in a week or so. And as the year-tens were back in school for a short spell, your correspondent had been allowed back to chat to one or two of them. Outside, needless to say, and from a suitable social distance.

"I'm missing football very much," Sukhra mused. At which point his class-mate Aneyaan Iqbal nodded assent. When I asked him what he'd missed most about school, the answer was "seeing friends, sharing jokes, playing football".

Aneeyan is fourteen and lives in Handsworth. Both parents came from Pakistan. "Dad handles complaints for a gas company and Mum's a teaching assistant," he told me.

Yes, he agreed with Sukhra that the school had been helpful in setting work on-line. "But it's been a very different environment. You haven't had teachers there to support you. Instead you've had to email them. Still, the school have emailed daily updates and phoned home at regular intervals to check that I'm okay."

Anayaan had arrived at Lordswood from another school last September. "Immediately I was made very welcome here," he recalled. "I felt at home."

But at that time he didn't have to be at home, day in day out, for weeks upon end. "Once you've done the work set by the school, there hasn't been much else to do. The furthest I've been until now was the local park."

To see your mates?

"No. I've had to stay with the family, keeping far away from anyone else."

Time, perhaps, to talk to someone who has witnessed at first hand the lives of Lordswood lads with more than boredom to contend with during the lengthy lockdown. "I would be wrong to say that I'm not worried about the lasting impact on the more vulnerable students," the head had told me shortly before heading for Coventry.

"But the signs are that the ones we've had back into school at the moment have kept themselves well, and it doesn't look as though there's been any serious abuse of any kind at home. Still, we know that there are a small number of students who will have faced some quite adverse experiences over the past few months. We're learning about those as the weeks go on, aren't we?"

"Absolutely," confirmed Jane Thompson, to whom he'd just re-introduced me. Jane, or "Ms Thompson" as I should call her on school premises, teaches history and had just been telling me how much she'd enjoyed being back in the classroom, albeit for an hour or two – "being able to answer questions, correct any misunderstandings, and just have a bit of banter with the lads".

As I mentioned in the previous chapter, she's also an assistant headteacher and the lead safeguarding officer in the school. So during the lockdown she'd not only been teaching from home but having to visit the homes of others.

"We have an education welfare officer and she's done the vast majority of home visits," she told me. "But with some of our most needy students I've gone out to see them and their families." Indeed she found herself "doing a bit of shopping" for one family. "The mother was having to self-isolate and didn't have any family around to go to the shops for her. She's the mother of one of our year-seven kids and his eldest brother had been taken into care for violent behaviour."

It must be difficult to keep your "social distance" in those circumstances, I suggested.

"Yes, it is. When you're trying to build a relationship with families that have problems, it's frustrating not to be able to offer a handshake or see inside the property. I remember being at one house with a lot of people in a very confined space."

A white, British family, as it happened, from what used to be called the "working class".

"There was a lack of any routine or boundaries," Ms Thompson went on. "Obviously I wasn't able to go inside. But you only had to stand at the door or peer through the window to get a sense of what was going on. Sometimes our boys are with parents that don't value education. Those issues were already there, but the lockdown has thrown them into the spotlight.

"There are also issues around child protection in some cases. We have to keep checking that they're okay. Others have learning difficulties or ADHD (Attention Deficit Hyperactivity Disorder). Where we can, we've tried to help get them back into school. That's really helped the children and their families."

Some members of those families have gone down with the virus. Others have lost jobs because of it. "The financial effect of that has had a major impact." At this point the assistant head shook her head and sighed.

Earlier in our conversation I'd asked her, as a historian, if she could ever have imagined what would happen in the viral summer of 2020. Another shake of the head. "If you'd have said six months ago that we'd have this long off school, nobody would have believed it."

It had shown starkly "how much schools have to do beyond just education". Slight pause. "And this school's done more than most."

Like Lee Williams, Jane Thompson, now forty-one, grew up not far from "this school". Further west along the Hagley Road – in a police house, as it happened. Well, her father was one of the "boys in blue". Long retired and living in East Yorkshire, "Dad" is justifiably proud of a daughter whom he encouraged to study hard for qualifications. "Once you've got those pieces of paper," he'd told her, "nobody can take them away from you."

She got her critical "pieces of paper" from the sixth-form at King Edward's Five Ways (yes, my old grammar school) and at the University of Warwick, which just happens to be in Coventry.

Before returning to Birmingham's west side, she'd taught at Baverstock Academy in Druid's Heath, an area of the city dominated by what was once called a council estate. The academy was closed in 2017. "It was a real effort to get the parents involved and the kids engaged," she recalled. "Particularly the boys."

Nonetheless, she moved on to a boys' school – King's Norton, a former grammar school in a posher part of town, where she was head of the sixth-form as well as the history department.

So why go to Lordswood?

The chance to be an assistant head of a whole school for one thing; Director of School Improvement Michael Rennie for another. "Michael's passion for helping these boys came over during my interview," she recalled. "And when he told me what he wanted in terms of history teaching, I very much wanted to roll my sleeves up straight away. He really did sell the vision to me and he has very high expectations."

She soon became conscious too of the expectations of parents of boys who had only recently arrived on these shores. "They really value education as something transformative for these kids' lives," she mused before going on to say, "Whether they come from a rich or poor family, they deserve the same level of education. With my history lessons I aim for what I think is a high level. I sometimes use academic language and set challenging tasks while supporting those children that might struggle."

Since the lockdown, however, she has largely had to work from home. So has her oldest daughter, aged twelve, a student at King's Norton Girls' School. So has her husband who teaches at Five Ways. And so has her younger daughter, aged ten, who goes to St Laurence Primary close to the family home in Northfield.

That just happened to be the school where my short-trousered legs were once thrashed by a formidable ruler-wielding teacher called Mrs Rawlinson. My offence had been to flick ink over the immaculate handwriting of the girl who sat behind me. Our desks in those days still had inbuilt inkwells. And, in case you're wondering, the pen that I'd dipped before flicking was not a quill. It had a new-fangled italic nib attached to a stick rather than a feather.

The good old days, eh?

And, hey, that's enough of dwelling on my childhood some sixty summers or so ago.

What about the past served up to boys from many parts of the world by the history curriculum as laid down by Michael Gove as recently as 2013 when he was Secretary of State for Education?

"Under the Gove reforms there's a lot more British history," said Ms Thompson. "And you can't teach British history without bringing in the Empire."

Not easy when you're teaching predominantly black and Asian students in the wake of George Floyd's death at the hands (or rather the knee) of an American cop, and the subsequent demonstrations on both sides of the Atlantic. "I'm certainly going to have to take account of the Black Lives Matter movement," she confirmed.

So what would her stance be on the pulling down of statues?

"Errrmmm, I certainly understand why some demonstrators would want to pull them down. But those statues are also a useful way to confront some of the difficult issues about our past. History is always being reinterpreted and the George Floyd case may well be a good starting point to debate racism in this country in the past and how we can tackle it today."

Something to dwell on for tomorrow, perhaps. Or at least for September when there would – hopefully – be far more boys in school than just year-tens for two hours a day.

Lee Williams would have welcomed an Ofsted inspection this year

Chapter Ten

Not Too Great Expectations Greatly Exceeded

It was a miserable Monday morning. Despite being late July, it was drizzly and dreary as the traffic crawled through Small Heath on the east side of the inner-city. A century ago this would have been Peaky Blinders territory. Until, that is, other street gangs threatened the Peakies' pre-eminence. Successfully so in the case of the Birmingham Boys, led by one Billy Kimber.

As the somewhat glamorised BBC series pointed out, local outposts of Irish republicanism were part of the turbulent mix at the time. And Irish immigration into Birmingham continued in the decades that followed. Those from just "across the water" tended to settle on this side of a city that offered jobs a-plenty on building sites and road developments.

Today the population in and around Small Heath is predominantly Muslim. The Balti Belt is nearby, offering mouth-watering menus at very affordable prices. Halal butchers abound and fruit and veg stalls spill some colour on to the main street. Much needed colour on a day like today. Their customers were predominantly female, some with veils, some with face masks, some with both.

Meanwhile, the car crawled on and the windscreen wipers continued to swish. Just as Birmingham City's ground loomed into view, the sat-nav seemed to wake up and instructed me to turn right into Green Lane before bearing left into Little Green Lane.

You won't be surprised to hear that those "lanes" weren't quite as idyllic as they sounded. Victorian terraces, for the most part. Until, that is, I was told to turn left where I had finally reached my destination – a little cul-de-sac of social housing just across the border into Bordesley Green. Still terraced and "compact", as estate agents might have described them, albeit comparatively modern. Some even had roofs of solar panelling. Needless to say, there would be little of a solar nature coming their way today.

"Ours is the one with more panelling than anyone else," I was told by Haaris Saghir when I rang to tell him that I was here. Not that I would be going inside. Cases of Covid-19 had declined since their peak, but the virus was very much with us still.

At this point two men emerged from a road maintenance van parked nearby and started drilling. The juddering rumble that followed was hardly conducive to clarity on my voice recorder.

Thankfully, Haaris was able to lead the way to the "Common Room", which sounded like a gathering place for teachers but turned out to be a community centre. An empty one, what's more. We were able to converse from a suitable social distance with the voice recorder on the table between us.

Some readers may recall that I'd mentioned the name of Haaris Saghir in an earlier chapter. He was one of the Lordswood lads who exceeded all expectations. Passed all eight GCSEs, albeit after having to re-sit maths. But it was his English results that stood out. Predicted to get level-threes in language and literature, he came up with level-eights in each – or grade-As as they would have been called at one time.

"That was amazing," I told him. And I meant it. Honestly.

"Thanks," he said modestly from under his cap. A "cool" cap rather than a school cap, I should add. He would be eighteen in a couple of weeks and, thanks to the pandemic, his A-level results in language, literature and sociology would be based on continuous assessment rather than exams.

The lack of a sixth-form at his former school meant that he'd had to go elsewhere to study for them. Solihull College, as it happened. Was he disappointed not to have stayed at Lordswood?

"Oh yes."

Even though it's quite a way from here?

"I used to have to get a bus into town and another one out again. It took me a good hour in the morning and sometimes an hour and a half on the way back."

Which begged the question: why?

Obvious answer: because they had plenty of places for those who had arrived in the city comparatively recently. Haaris had come to Brum, aged eight, with his mother and two of his bothers. The older one, by "three or four years", had been readily accepted into Lordswood and he had felt inclined to follow suit after a short spell at a primary school closer to home.

The Saghirs (minus "Dad" and an even older brother, now twenty-five) had settled here in 2010. Not from Pakistan but from Banbury in Oxfordshire. As Haaris was starting to explain how and why, there was a knock on the Common Room door and his mother came in to join us. Over to you, Farah:

"I was born and bred in Birmingham," she told me in a distinctive but not broad Brummie accent. "This is my home. But I had to move to Banbury when I got married in 1992."

It was an arranged marriage and it formally ended with a civil divorce eighteen years later. "We were separated before that," she recalled. "I didn't take to Banbury," she added with some feeling. "It was very much a small town and I didn't even like the water."

How could it compete with the soft, Welsh nectar pumped from the Elan Valley to Birmingham since the days when Joseph Chamberlain ran the City Council? Still, I suspect that there was more behind the marriage break-up than the content of Banbury's taps. Time, perhaps, to move the subject of Haaris's unexpected GCSE successes. Was she proud?

"Very," she beamed with an adoring smile in her son's direction. Farah was all too evidently a devoted mother. But she was contemplating going back to her former job in the office of a bank now that the lockdown was easing somewhat. When I suggested that it couldn't have been easy living with three boys in a small space for months on end, the answer came with another smile and a hint of nervous laughter:

"The routine was upside down and they were going to bed late. Otherwise it was fine."

Only one member of the family had gone down with the virus, it seemed. "My cousin's a doctor and he obviously caught it from a patient," Farah explained. "But he's okay now," she assured me before dropping out that she had a brother with a PhD from Oxford University. "Can't remember the subject now. It was a long time ago."

All the same, doctorates in philosophy and medicine among close relatives suggested that there was no shortage of brainpower in the family.

Haaris's brainpower was none too evident during his early years at Lordswood. "A lot of kids seemed to find school fun," he recalled. "They were just messing around. Because we were never really pushed, it was hard to work in that environment. But things started to get better when I reached year-nine."

Readers won't be surprised to know that the coming of the CAT, otherwise known as the Central Academies Trust, had something to do with it – or rather everything to do with it. "Miss Rennie and Mr Rennie made the big difference," Haaris mused.

"Miss" Rennie, otherwise known as Clare or "the Lionel Messi of the classroom", left a lengthy impact during her short time at Lordswood where her father Michael is still Director of School Improvement [see chapters six and seven]. "She used to say that she saw potential in me," Haaris went on. "And that kind of boosted my confidence. I used to go to extra classes with her at lunchtimes. Got some Amazon vouchers for just turning up, but I would have gone anyway. I've now got a passion for English literature."

The syllabus included William Blake and Robert Louis Stevenson. Plus Shakespeare, of course. Not forgetting JB Priestley's *An Inspector Calls*, set in a fictional Midland town called "Brumley". Or, indeed, the First World War poets. "I particularly liked the works of Wilfred Owen and others," he reflected. "Read a whole anthology of them."

So here was a lad of Pakistani heritage, born in the 21st century, enthusing about a poet who died eighteen years into the last century. That says much about the quality of the teaching that he received. For a very traditionally English literary syllabus, it must be said.

Not that Clare Rennie felt that his heritage had anything to do with it. After all, he was born and brought up in England. "It was rather," she told me, "that he was able to quickly and effectively analyse complex poetic devices and themes completely naturally."

All the same, doing A-levels at Solihull had not been easy. "I found it a big step up," he admitted. But his ambition to go to law school and become a solicitor remained. Not that he planned to leave home any time soon. "I like living in this city," he shrugged. "So if I don't get into Birmingham University, I'm hoping to go to Aston."

It all depended on the assessment of how he would have done in his A-levels had he been able to sit exams. We'd know soon enough. Results day was just over two weeks away.

Fingers crossed, Haaris. And I meant that. Honestly.

The following day dawned brighter and breezier. I was heading back towards Lordswood, and a bit beyond. To Lightwoods Park, as it happened – a great swathe of greenery lining the other side of the Hagley Road and beautifying the borough of Sandwell. Well, part of it.

Smethwick was nearby, where Denis Brinzei lived in a terraced street similar to the one where Headteacher Lee Williams had grown up in the '80s and '90s.

Denis had arrived in the UK from Romania six years ago. He couldn't speak a word of English. Now, on the basis of his mock exams and course work, he was expected to achieve decent GCSE pass grades in language and literature. Maths too.

We'd know for sure on August 20 when we were both planning to be at the school across the road with others whose last year at Lordswood had been disrupted by the viral intruder known as Corona.

The need to keep a social distance apart, preferably in the open air, was the reason why we'd arranged to meet in the park rather than the nearby house where Denis lived with his mother Ana (a hairdresser), his "stepdad" Ioan Balan (a delivery driver) and his much younger brother, aged two.

I'd arrived a little early for our meeting, so I parked myself on a picnic bench near the bandstand and opposite what is known locally as "the big house" – an imposing 18th century mansion now housing Jonathan's Restaurant. Next door was the walled "Shakespeare Garden". Apparently it's full of plants mentioned in the works of the Bard.

You could set your sundial by the way that Denis came striding across the greensward cometh the appointed hour. He was sporting earphones, which he duly removed, and reflective sunglasses that seemed to hold a mirror up to whatever or whoever was in his sights. Me in this case. Looking positively ancient, it must be said, compared to this strapping teenager who seemed polite, confident and charming. Well-spoken too, considering that not so long ago he was in classes for those with English as a second language.

Not that they taught him much, either at primary school near his mother's first English home in Bearwood or during a brief spell living across town in Small Heath when Baverstock was his first experience of secondary education. Not a good one either. As mentioned in the previous chapter, the former "academy" was closed down in 2017. Just as well, as far as Denis was concerned. "If I'd had to depend on that place, I wouldn't have had any English when I left school," he mused.

Lordswood accepted him – "they'd accept anybody" – four years ago. "At that time," he went on, "we had so many teachers on almost every subject. They seemed to change every three weeks.

"Everything started to change when I was in year-nine. I had teachers who encouraged me and showed me that I had a lot of potential. I started to think 'hey, I want a good life. I want a nice house and car. And a stable family.'

"My grades started improving. I remember getting my first grade two and was so excited. Then, oh my God, I got a grade three. Now I'm getting fives and sixes, even sevens sometimes."

Lordswood had really started to change half way through year-ten when the aforesaid Smethwick-born-and-bred "Mr Williams" had been appointed Headteacher.

"He was seen as quite strict and some kids started saying that 'school's going to be horrible'," Denis recalled. "To be honest, though, everybody's grades started going up. And it started to make a massive difference to my chances. In maths in year-eleven, for instance, I moved from grades two and three to five."

And Mr Williams?

"He taught me graphic design and really inspired me. That's what I've been focused on during the lockdown. It's one of the subjects that I want to focus on in the sixth-form, hopefully at Matthew Boulton College. Then I want to do it at Coventry University. They came to Lordswood to do a very good presentation of what it would be like there."

It couldn't have been easy for him, I suggested, coming from Romania during the build-up to Brexit and the anti-immigration sourness that swirled around it. But Denis was adamant. "I now feel that the UK is my home. People can have their own opinions. It's freedom of speech. As for kids at school, they can be the cruellest people. You just brush it off."

As we bade farewell and he strode off, I sensed again that growing self-confidence. Here was a kid who'd been given the chance to build a new life in a new country. It all depended on those GCSE results.

Once again, fingers crossed.

Denis Brinzei complete with reflective sun glasses

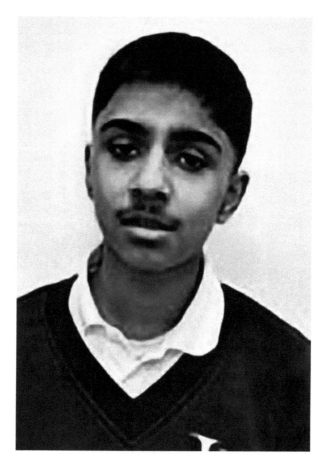

Haaris Saghir in his Lordswood days

Chapter Eleven

Celebration after Months of Isolation

It just so happened that Lee Williams was on his annual pilgrimage to the Pyrenees. With his wife Kelly, I should add, three children and five bikes. The lockdown had been eased on either side of the Channel, but cases were rising again.

It was August, the height of the holiday season, when the UK Government decided to impose a fortnight in quarantine on those travelling home from France.

"We were due back twenty four hours after the four am deadline," the head of Lordswood Boys had sighed down the phone when we finally made contact. "I'd been on-line to try and change it but we were about two hundred and eighty ninth in the queue."

An eleven and a half hour overnight drive to Boulogne in the hope of acquiring a ticket for an earlier journey through the Channel Tunnel had proved futile. And such was the swarm of homebound Brits and the lack of social distancing that the Williamses decided to be tested for Covid-19 "for peace of mind" when they finally arrived back in Brum.

The results were negative yet the quarantine rule remained in force. "We'd just have to deal with it," Lee went on. "Kelly works remotely from home and I don't have to be back in my office."

The start of the new school year was still over two weeks away. However, there was one August morning when he would have loved to have been at Lordswood.

GCSE results day was going to be a time for celebration rather than trepidation for the vast majority of the boys. Thankfully, the furore over A-level results and the fiasco that followed had led to the abandonment of Ofqual's downgrading algorithm. Grades would be awarded by teaching staff on the basis of their mocks and their continuous assessment – the best grades by far for a school that had been in crisis only a few years previously. "Way above the national average," I'd been told by Michael Rennie, the aptly named Director of School Improvement.

"Truly remarkable, individually and collectively," Lee, or rather Mr Williams, told the accumulators of those grades in a video sent to every year-eleven student. "We are incredibly proud of you," he assured them. "And you should be incredibly proud of yourselves."

He looked forward to inviting them back to Lordswood for a collective celebration in the – hopefully – "not too distant future".

At least his deputy Rajdip Kang was there to give a warm welcome to those year-elevens when they returned for the first time in many a month. There as well were assistant heads Jane Thompson and Lindsay Greatrix. Not forgetting subject team leaders for English and Music Kiran Sandhu and Marie Lowndes-Ford, both due to begin the fast-approaching new term as Assistant Headteachers.

It seemed like an eternity since Ms L-F had shown me around her expansive music room at the "new" Lordswood Boys' back in mid-March, just before the lockdown. Clad in a summery outfit, she seemed steadfastly oblivious to the sharp wind whipping down the side of the new school as she sat at a temporary table handing out registration forms. So breathy was the breeze that the forms had to be held in place buy a selection of Oxford mini-dictionaries.

Once registered, students could stroll a few yards or so across the tarmac to another table to hand them over to the school's attendance officer Ruksana Bi. "We need to know what they're planning next," she told me. "That's why we need full contact details. Don't forget that some of them will have moved home since March. Once they hand in these forms then I can give them what they've come for."

Celebration after Months of Isolation

Their results were neatly packed in little plastic folders from which they had to be plucked with trembling fingers. Or so I imagined. As it turned out, there wasn't much trembling in evidence. A key priority for sixteen-year-olds is to look "cool" in front of your mates.

Take Malvin Omali, for instance. He came originally from Nigeria, arrived here just over three years ago and lived in Handsworth with his parents. They were both with him today – almost in tears in the case of his mother who kept repeating "excellent, excellent" every time that her son matter-of-factly told her one exceptional grade after another.

There were sixes in history, English language and literature, a seven in chemistry, eights in maths and physics and a nine in biology.

As his science teacher, Raj was understandably delighted. "I want to give you a great big hug but I can't," she told modest Malvin, who seemed intent on playing it all down.

Dad, on the other hand, seemed intent on lifting him up. That's just what he did at one point, as though his son had just scored a winner for the Villa. Back on the ground once more, the strapping lad told me that he wanted to go into medicine. First he was going to do the sciences at A-level at Handsworth Grammar School. "He's got in already," Mum put in.

And as Malvin sloped off to chat to his mates, Dad smiled with pride. "He's just made my day," he beamed. "Can't wait to start celebrating. I feel like taking him to the moon and back." Then he broke off and switched towards addressing Raj and her colleagues. "I can't thank you enough," he told them with all too evident sincerity.

Jane duly called Malvin back for a family photo. "You're completely in the shade," she pointed out. "It's time to move into the sun."

Which seemed somehow symbolic, come to think of it.

Someone else with what should be a sunny future ahead of him was heading up the steps in a blue track-suit top with "Under Armour" written across it. That's "Armour" with an "r" rather than "Amour". And, yes, it's some kind of sportswear brand. Or so I was told.

Junayd Shamraze looked slightly embarrassed as the teachers gathered round, albeit at a suitable social distance. They knew what he didn't know yet: that he had a grade four in German, sixes in geography and religious education, two sevens in English language and literature, an eight in maths and two more eights and a seven in the three sciences.

"How's it going?" Raj asked breezily.

No audible answer. Not yet anyway. He set off at a brisk pace down the steps before I could get a word with him. "Don't worry. He's only gone to ring his parents," the deputy head assured me. "He'll be back."

And he was, his face breaking into a small smile as he slipped the phone into his tracksuit pocket. Needless to say, his parents would have been delighted. One's an engineer at Birmingham University, the other a part-time carer, and they live across the Hagley Road on the Bearwood borders with Smethwick. Their own parents were from Pakistan.

Junayd was not one to talk about himself too much, it transpired.

"You've done well," I said.

"Yeah."

"Exceptionally well."

"Yeah, yeah."

"What are you going to do now?"

"Biology, chemistry and maths."

"Where?"

"Over there," he said, gesturing across the playing fields beyond towards Lordswood Girls' School. Lordswood boys were allowed in to the girls' sixth-form, it would seem, because they didn't have one of their own. But surely that will have to change soon if the past three years of unprecedented progress are anything to go by.

"We do need to start thinking about how we're going to grow that side of school," Raj agreed. "Most of the boys want to stay on here and the girls' school is the only option nearby."

Like Junayd, Vrutik Gohel was bound for the sixth-form a little further down the Harborne side of the posh Lordswood Road. Yet he lived in Oldbury on "the other side of the tracks", otherwise known as the Hagley Road. "Dad works in a factory and Mum doesn't go out to work," he told me when the congratulations of his teachers had finally died down. His grades were impressive, to put it mildly – nothing under a six, plus eights in English language and biology.

Now he wanted to do A-levels in applied science, computer science and IT. Computers certainly seem to have worked well for him during the lockdown. "Sometimes I missed being at school," he shrugged, "but I had no trouble doing the work on-line."

As Vrutik strolled off, I spotted another evidently proud mother whose smile could have lit up a Test Match in Southampton. "I'm Dylan Cassidy's Mum. He's passed all seven and got an eight in history," she told me. "And he hasn't lived here long. Only came back from Norway last year."

Norway?

That seemed unusual, even by Lordswood standards.

"He was living over there with his father, who's a hotel worker."

"And you?"

"I work for the traffic police. Live down the road in Quinton. And I'm absolutely ecstatic about Dylan's results," she added with some feeling before pointing out her son chatting to some friends nearby. "That's Dylan; the one with the bottle."

A water bottle, in case you're wondering. He was still clutching it as he wandered over in our direction after a summons from Mum. "Yeah, I've done okay," he grinned and seemed particularly pleased about that eight in history. "That's what I want to do at A-level, along with a few other things. It would have been good to do it here."

Ah well. Halesowen College seemed to be the next option. Only three and a half miles from Quinton, but a very long way from Norway.

"I went there for a holiday when I was a child and decided to stay there with my Dad," he explained before going on to say that "my Mum has really helped me settle down back in Birmingham. I'm quite happy here now."

Norway to Quinton seemed almost as incongruous as Romania to Smethwick. What on earth had happened to Denis Brinzei, the Romanian lad who'd arrived in this country with his mother six years ago? "Without a word of English," he'd confirmed when we'd met across the way in Lightswood Park [see Chapter Ten].

He'd also confirmed then that he would be at Lordswood for his GCSE results on what might be called the "early shift" – the group of boys booked in for 8.30 am. Accordingly I'd been up at the crack of dawn and driven quite a way for what could be Denis's big day.

As it transpired, he finally arrived around 9.45.

No matter. I'd heard plenty of intriguing tales in the meantime, and Denis knew how to make an entrance. He was still some distance away when he stopped dead and threw open his arms to greet his teachers with what would no doubt have been a broad grin had he not been wearing a mask, like many another student. The teachers waved back enthusiastically.

Such was the strength of the wind that he had trouble separating the sheets when he finally reached Ruksana's table and prised his results from the plastic packaging. "Look at the second page, Denis," Raj urged him.

He did, eventually, and then let rip with a resounding "yesss, a six", as though he'd just hit one. In fact, he'd achieved a grade six in his all-important graphics. (Thanks, Mr Williams.)

Then came "four and five in language and literature", followed by a short pause to take it in. "Wow! That's okay." More than "okay", I would have thought, bearing in mind that we're talking about English language and literature for a lad who'd spent the first ten of his sixteen years in Romania.

Denis went on reading his results. Grade four in maths and five in geography – or it might have been photography. The wind was playing havoc with my voice recorder. But I couldn't miss the excited screech that followed.

"How did I get a four in science?" he asked rhetorically before going on to say, "The only thing I've failed at his health and fitness. Never mind that. I'm okay. Really happy, I certainly didn't expect that result in science, let alone maths and English. I think my Mum will be proud. And my step-dad."

His teachers should be proud too – proud of themselves for transforming the chances of a lad who could all too easily have been written off as a no-hoper.

At that point I remembered Haaris Saghir, whom we also met in the last chapter. Like Denis, his chances had been "changed, changed utterly" by the takeover of Lordswood by the Central Academies Trust. Were they now about to be ruined by that wretched algorithm?

By his own admission Haaris had found A-levels at Solihull College quite a "step-up". But he'd still been expected to be awarded Bs and

Cs. Instead Ofqual had downgraded him. Or "ungraded" him in the case of sociology, for which he'd been given a "U". It might as well stand for "useless". What's more, they'd handed him two Es in his beloved English literature and language.

Haaris was understandably upset when I finally got hold of him on the phone.

Since then, however, there had been a U-turn. A-level results, like GCSEs, would be restored to predictions based on course work. Ofqual chairman Roger Taylor, meanwhile, had threatened to resign after being blamed, he claimed, by the Education Secretary Gavin Williamson.

That's the same Gavin Williamson, incidentally, who used to be Chief Whip and liked to brag about the tarantula that he apparently kept on his desk. The same Gavin Williamson who appeared on television with a ghastly grin to reassure students and parents that everything would be all right. The same Gavin Williamson who had offered to resign shortly afterwards – only to be turned down by the Prime Minister who had appointed him, no doubt with the approval of his string-puller ... sorry, chief of staff, Dominic Cummings.

A few days later it was Sally Collier, Ofqual's chief regulator, who did resign.

Farce?

Fiasco?

The words hardly seemed adequate for the likes of Haaris who had been offered a bright future only to see the light turned right down.

Back at Lordswood his brother Humza had just slipped in to pick up his GCSE results. Unlike Denis, he seemed a quiet and undemonstrative lad. Mind you, his results did raise a hint of a smile. There were fives in English language and literature as well as PE, sixes in maths, history and one of his sciences. A four and a five in the others.

"So what are you going to do now?"

"Er ... sixth form."

"At?"

"Lordswood Girls."

Business studies, science and maths, apparently. "You've done well," I went on. "Quite a few sixes."

"Yeah."

"Looking forward to telling your Mum?"

"Yeah."

That response was sounding somewhat familiar. I hadn't heard quite so many "yeahs" since the early days of the Beatles

No matter. Perhaps it was time to let Humza head off home. After all he had two buses to catch on his trek across town to Bordesley Green where his older brother had resumed his part-time and, hopefully, temporary job in a gym.

Haaris's A-levels had finally been upgraded. They were still disappointing, however, for a lad of his intelligence. He was given three Ds. Having told me this over the phone, he then dropped out that he had been involved in a car crash in October, 2019, a couple of months or so before taking his mocks.

"I had a fractured nose but my mate was nearly paralysed," he revealed. "He's made a good recovery, but that crash had a traumatic effect on me. I've never completely recovered."

"Did your A-level teachers know about that?"

"Yes. And I thought they understood what I'd been going through."

He was now planning to re-sit, probably through Solihull College. That's what his mother, Farah, wants him to do. "I was quite upset when those grades were confirmed," she told me in a separate phone conversation. "Haaris had tears in his eyes when he told me."

And, yes, she did think that he was still affected by being involved that crash some ten months ago. "He always seems nervous whenever he gets into the passenger seat," she mused.

Our conversation had been a sobering comedown after a joyful morning of GCSE results at Lordswood. Now the uncertainties of a new school year beckoned, with Covid-19 still a present and future threat. Particularly so in Birmingham where cases were rising. The city had been put on the Government's "watch-list". Apart from anything else, it would mean that pupils would be expected to wear face masks in corridors and other communal areas – on rotas or in bubbles, depending on troubles.

The same Government, mind you, kept assuring us that getting children back to school was a priority. On that promise at least, we could only hope that there would be no more U-turns.

****

Those of you who read Chapter Four may be wondering how James Cheam-Smith fared in the Eton equivalent of A-levels. He was the lad, you may recall, who was accepted into the most prestigious of public schools after winning a scholarship from Lordswood Boys.

"Originally I was downgraded a tiny bit – in German of all things!" he told me by email.

Not for long, it would seem. His final results were as follows: German D2, English D3 and music M1. Translated into common-or-garden A-levels that means a high A* in German, and A*/A in English and an A/B in music.

His offer from Lancaster University had been unconditional anyway. He was "very excited" about moving up there. Very different from Eton, that's for sure. And very different from how it was "in my day", as northerners used to say.

Best of luck, James. Hope you enjoy Saturday nights out in Lancaster and indeed in nearby Morecambe – a sharp contrast with Windsor.

Stop Press: *Never mind re-sitting at Solihull College. Despite his disappointing A-level results, Haaris Saghir was belatedly accepted by Wolverhampton University to study law*

Malvin Omani and very proud parents

Celebration after Months of Isolation

Denis Brinzei looking justifiably proud

Putting the flags out for Lordswood

Senior staff awaiting the "first shift "

Dylan Cassidy and his very happy Mum

Lee Williams, Head of School, Lordswood Boys' School

A self-isolating Mr Williams sending his congratulations via video

Chapter Twelve

Keeping Calm and Carrying On

Some hundred and eighty boys had been at school all of two days when they were sent home again. As it turned out, they didn't have to be. The Department for Education was being somewhat overcautious.

The saga began when long-time Lordswood receptionist Jasbinder Thandi took a call from a mother who could hardly speak a word of English. Luckily, Jas is fluent in Punjabi. She was told that the father of a lad who'd just started in year seven had tested positive for the Corona virus. He was promptly sent home – the lad that is, as well as his dad. "Every one of the staff at the company where father worked caught the virus," according to Jas. Birmingham City Council has since closed it down.

Following due procedure, the school informed Birmingham's public health department and – when they finally got through – the Department for Education. The initial response amounted to "send them home". Not just the boy who had already been sent home. And not just his fellow year-sevens, but year-eights as well.

"Soon afterwards we had a call back from the D f E to say that we shouldn't be sending all those children home. We should wait until the boy himself had been tested. Well, now he has and, no, he hasn't got the virus. So years seven and eight are back today."

That was David Kershaw talking. Through a mask, I might add. We were both be-masked as the chief executive of the Central Academies Trust drove us towards the west side of Birmingham, just as he had nine months previously when I'd started this book in what now felt like a different era. I know I've used the term "BC" before, but it seems an appropriate abbreviation for those distant days Before Corona.

119

The virus had been on the rise in Brum during the summer months. The city was now on the Government's "watch list" for a potential Leicester-like lockdown.

"To be fair to the D f E, they're under a lot of pressure and somebody had just made a mistake," said the man who'd been appointed by the Government's education department in 2017 to sort out Lordswood Boys – as he had many another failing school since his days as head of Coundon Court in Coventry.

Three years on and the Trust's transformation of LBS had brought forth Government money for a brand new building. Its 1950s fore-runner had finally been flattened.

Now here we were on a Friday morning in September pulling up just past a swathe of brand new basketball courts that had been covered with bulldozers and diggers on my last visit, just three weeks previously.

David had two meetings. One was about getting psychological support for those boys who'd been mentally affected by being locked out of Lordswood for six months. "The very nature of the school means that there's always a group of vulnerable youngsters," he'd reminded me on the way here. "So we hire a trained psychologist to give them support with their emotional development. It's something we've been trialling for twelve months with three or four boys and their families."

Today's meeting was to look at ways of extending that help. Although no Lordswood boys had caught the virus (so far), its effects were hardly confined to the physical. "Since the start of term there's been evidence that some students have gone unusually quiet. It could easily be a dozen and probably nearer twenty," he'd added.

His other meeting was about human resources – a key issue at Lordswood since so many teachers had been moved on and so many more taken on. "We're developing a relationship with a specialist HR company so that we can free up our senior staff to spend more time on educational issues," he said.

"Dr Kershaw" himself had agreed not to go anywhere near the "youngsters" during his time at Lordswood. He is, after all, seventy-seven years old and therefore considered vulnerable to any potential infection.

Despite being a spring chicken of seventy-one, I wasn't planning to get too close to any students either. I did, though, have an appointment with the Headteacher in his new office.

First question: where's the coffee machine? I'd been looking forward to a good strong Americano of the sort that Lee Williams had presented me with on my first visit to his old office in the old school in the old days, BC or PP: pre-pandemic.

"I've had to stop drinking coffee," the head confided. "I was having too many cups during the lockdown and getting severe headaches as a consequence."

There was a box of tea bags on top of the fridge and, after I'd declined the offer of a "cuppa", he made one for himself. In a large mug decorated with images of the First World War, as it happened. That came as no surprise. On the short walk from the car park you couldn't help but notice that the new Tarmac footpaths were emblazoned with war-time references in large, white capital letters:

"LEST WE FORGET," said one. "1st JULY, 1916," said another, pinpointing the first bloody day of many in the Battle of the Somme.

"The intention is to act as a constant reminder of the sacrifices that our ancestors have made," Lee explained before going on to tell me that the school has had an annual trip every summer to a place near the German-English front line. "There's a small B&B there and we've developed a good relationship with them on previous visits," he went on. And, yes, the school was hoping to make another trip next summer. "Hopefully things will have changed by then."

A fascination with the First World War is just one of the interests that the Headteacher shares with the Director of School Improvement, Michael Rennie. The others are American football and baseball. In fact, a baseball was nestling next to the hand sanitiser on his desk.

But cycling remains the main sporting passion of Mr Williams, as I should be calling him now that a new school year had finally begun. It was time to get down to basics and ask how things had been going – apart from the farce over years seven and eight being sent home for two days on Government orders.

Well, the staff were all back, it seemed, joined by the new recruits. And Michael Rennie's daughter Clare, otherwise known as "the Lionel Messi of the classroom", had made a welcome return for four days a week, albeit only for a month or so.

Not all the Lordswood boys had returned, however.

"There are about seven whose parents have decided that they're not going to send their sons back," the head said. "We can't do much about it, apart from report their absence to the educational welfare officer and keep sending them classroom material on-line."

Why are they still being kept at home?

"The parents aren't worried about our protocols; they're just worried about their sons going out at all while infection rates are going up again."

Talking of protocols, how were safety measures being enforced for the vast majority who were back at their desks?

"Only each year-group bubble can be in a particularly assigned classroom. And students don't move classrooms between lessons now." Which explained why I'd heard no clatter and chatter in the corridors whenever the hooter tooted.

"Instead the teachers move to the students," Mr Williams went on. "We've also purchased visors for every student as well as every teacher.

They're compulsory in the classrooms. And masks are mandatory anywhere else in the school. Unless they're eating, of course."

Separate staircases and corridors had been assigned for each year-group bubble. All the same, I pointed out, these measures can't be enforced once the boys are off school premises.

"No, they can't. As soon as they go through the gate, it stops. That's the main concerning issue around the return to school"

Did he get the impression, talking to the kids, that most of them are glad to be back in school?

"A hundred per cent, without a doubt. They've missed school and everything about it."

Some had been quite adversely affected by the lockdown, I suggested, recalling what I'd been told on the journey here this morning.

"Yes, there have been some adverse effects," he acknowledged. "To be honest, though, we've not witnessed anything too concerning. But we know that there are students out there who've had a worse time than others," he added before going on to say, "These times are testing enough. The distance between pupils and the school over the past six months has been significant. We have to ensure that the staff, and the leadership team in particular, step back into the ethos of the school as it was. It's a matter of being organised and positive in the messages that are given out, and not to shy away from ensuring that standards are maintained."

Or, to quote from slogan coined when another world war was about to break out, "Keep calm and carry on".

Shortly before carrying on to the Kershaw meeting on human resources, the head had disclosed that Haaris Saghir had called in at his old school the day before. Maybe he'd heard that Clare Rennie was briefly back teaching at Lordswood.

It was Clare, after all, who had inspired him to achieve two grade eights in English language and literature instead of the grade threes that had been predicted.

As mentioned in the previous chapter, his A-level grades from Solihull College had been comparatively disappointing. Still, he was now heading for Wolverhampton University to read law.

Haaris must have been somewhat chuffed to see his name on the Lordswood "Hall of Fame", attached to a wall in what is now called the "refectory". There were two names above Haaris's, also embossed in gold on a dark brown background.

One was James Smith, honoured for his "exceptional academic achievements, including Eton scholarship (2018)". The other, right at the top, was Jasbinder Thandi for "38 years of loyal and dedicated service".

Thirty eight years?

That meant that she would have begun working here in 1982 when Mike Gayle, "No. 1 bestselling author", was a first-year pupil. His name was at the bottom of this roll of honour, just below Paul Tilsley who is described as the "first cohort student at Lordswood Boys' School (1957)". Oh yes and "Lord Mayor of Birmingham (1993-94)".

So tell us, Jas, what was Lordswood like when you (and Mike Gayle) started here nearly four decades ago?

"It was mainly English teachers and English pupils."

Not all of them white English, it would seem. Mike Gayle himself was born up the road in Quinton but both his parents were from Jamaica. And being black didn't stop him becoming head boy, even back in those days.

Nonetheless, the school has changed, changed and changed again over the nigh-on four decades since Jas started work here. Now here she was taking me for a last look around, just as she had given me my first tour round the old school nearly nine months ago, BC.

One thing hadn't changed in that seemingly interminable time. Alex Nyarko, who'd started teaching in Ghana, still had his maths class listening in studious silence as he explained and demonstrated formulae that would have had me flummoxed.

No doubt head of English Kiran Sandhu, whom I'd met on the same seemingly distant day, would be holding forth elsewhere on William Blake or Wilfred Owen. Or even the Bard himself.

It just so happened that Jas and I were in the corridor outside when another English teacher was telling her class, with theatrical projection, how Juliet had faked her death. There was a dramatic pause when you could have heard a quill drop. "She wakes up . . . "

Yes, we know what happens next. Well, some of us do. Not all these lads, judging by their rapt attention. Mouths might have been agape behind those masks and visors.

Nearby, a history teacher spotted us and popped out to talk. Victoria Bone turned out to be one of the new recruits that had joined the staff during the lockdown. "This is year-eight history," she told me in another voice that resonated, despite the visor. "We've just started mediaeval Britain. Not looking at kings and queens, mind you, but the lives of ordinary people."

Historical dates were highlighted on the walls – not in the classroom but round every corridor down which Jas and I strolled. Everything from the Great Fire of London (1666) to England winning the World Cup three hundred years later. Plus a lot more in between and either side.

For the first time in my life I saw an oblique connection between John Lennon (1940 to '80) and Malcolm X (1925 to '65). Both had been shot in New York City forty years after their birth. And, in MX's case, exactly nine days after he had been in Smethwick proclaiming against the all-too-rampant racism of the time.

Jas remembered that racism all too well. And I remember writing about it in Chapter Two. She'd told me how she and her sister were "ignored as if we were nobodies" when they put up their hands to answer questions in the classroom.

Now her name is atop a "Hall of Fame" in a school on the posh side of the Hagley Road – a school that you had to pass the eleven-plus to get into when she was growing up.

Well, here's to you, Jas. And here's to the Trust that transformed that school after it declined into an institution that was failing boys shipped in from much poorer parts of the city.

Here's to the teaching staff whose skill and dedication has inspired so many of those boys to make something of their lives against the odds. And here's to the boys themselves, some of whom I've had the chance to chat to.

Much of this year has not been easy for them, their families and for many more families all over the country whose lives have been devastated by the virus.

Nobody knew what was going to happen next, or even whether schools would be allowed to stay open. Still, as we strolled to the car park up a path lined with the words LEST WE FORGET, I glanced back for one last look at a building that I'll always remember – a building that offered hope for a better future.

One of these days.

HALL OF FAME

Jasbinder Thandi
38 years loyal and dedicated service

James Smith
Exceptional academic achievements including
Eton scholarship (2018)

Haaris Saghir
Remarkable academic achievements in English Language
and English Literature (2018)

Paul Tilsley
First cohort student at Lordswood Boys' School (1957)
Lord Mayor of Birmingham (1993-94)

Mike Gayle
No.1 bestselling author, a student at Lordswood Boys'
School 1982-1989

The Lordswood Hall of Fame in the refectory

Lest we Forget. How could we?

Date of the first day of the Battle of the Somme

On guard outside the school

Biography

Chris Arnot has written twelve non-fiction books. *Small Island by Little Train* was published by the AA in 2017 and shortlisted for the Edward Stanford awards for travel writing the following year. Marcus Berkmann called it "very much a state-of-the-nation book" in his *Daily Mail* review.

Chris also wrote four of the Britain's Lost series for Aurum. *Britain's Lost Cricket Grounds* was reprinted twice after some glowing reviews. The late Frank Keating described it as "a coffee-table classic for and of posterity" in *The Guardian* and Jim Holden hailed it as "the best sports book of 2011" in the *Sunday Express*. Billy Elliot creator Lee Hall called *Britain's Lost Mines* "an extraordinary gallery of lives and landscapes".

As a national freelance journalist for a quarter of a century or so, Chris wrote for the *Guardian*, the *Independent*, the *Observer*, the *Times* and the *Telegraph*. And he's still a contributor to the *Sunday Telegraph*'s Pint to Pint column, a collection of which was published in hardback in 2016.

This is his fourth book for Takahe, including *Thanks Shanks: how Bill Shankly bought me an education*, which he ghost-wrote for David Kershaw – a prominent figure in Lordswood Boys' School's transformation from Decline and Fall to Rise and Shine.

Lightning Source UK Ltd.
Milton Keynes UK
UKHW020446261120
374086UK00002B/4

9 781908 837165